The Mystical Accord

The Mystical Accord

Sutras to Suit our Times
Lines for Spiritual Evolution

JAMES TUNNEY

ISBN 9781092324137

To Jennifer

Contents

Mystic accord,

way, vocation, path,

open up, feel it and fear not.

———————————

Millions of war ghosts

press against the pane of presence

to admonish.

———————————

Spirit is silkie on land

seeking and knowing

the sea is sought.

If you use magic beans

to make a stalk

you will have to slay giants.

———————————————

Spirit is the human

insufflation of the

cosmic consciousness.

———————————————

There are many ways

to the Way and many

ways away are there.

Gateway

"The Mystical in Art, the Mystical in Life, the Mystical in Nature,
that is what I am looking for."
Oscar Wilde, De Profundis

What is Mysticism?

The adjective 'mystical' in the title relates to mysticism and this is how I see it. Mysticism is a strange concept to many. The dictionaries are not always consistent nor helpful which creates a difficulty with operational definition, just as with other words such as 'natural.' The main senses of the word in Greek and Latin and associated languages suggest something that is hidden and something requiring initiation, perhaps closed and definitely mysterious. By looking at the origin of the word, usage and associated practices, we can identify possible meanings of the concept. I would suggest that various features of mysticism recur depending on the circumstances. Specification depends on such contexts and may involve a combination of characteristics. It may manifest as a philosophy, practice, disposition, tendency, attitude or way of life. I believe that mysticism really is an encompassing domain for areas now seen as distinct. Here are 10 possible elements, meanings or descriptions of mysticism that can be justified, separately or in combination, if you examine the history of the use of the term.

1. Mysticism relates to the metaphysical and to deep mysteries associated with things we cannot yet understand nor fully comprehend.

2. Mysticism is about an inner path to enlightenment, holiness and holism, sacredness, individual spiritual experience, growth and a unifying vision.

3. Mysticism is about an effort to encounter, apprehend, achieve spiritual union or come to the awareness of presence with the highest, transcendent, ultimate or cosmic consciousness, superconsciousness or God.

4. Mysticism is about secret, hidden, closed, esoteric doctrines, practices, initiation and mysteries related to the meaning of life.

5. Mysticism deals with direct engagement and exploration of consciousness, concepts of reality, imagination and other dimensions.

6. Mysticism is about inspiration, revelation and an alternative form of access to knowledge, reality and truth.

7. Mysticism involves an altered or enhanced state of consciousness often with access to non-local consciousness.

8. Mysticism may involve and be motivated by encounters and interaction with non-human beings or sources of intelligence and the supernatural.

9. Mysticism may seek to transcend the limits of words, reason, rationality and normal perception.

10. Mysticism is associated with opening a door of perception which leads to a denial of exclusivity of the common or normal view of material reality and standard ways of perceiving it.

There is a secondary meaning or definition, which uses 'mystic' or 'mystical' as a term of abuse associated with misty and foggy thinking, covering everything from superstition to New Age vagueness. This tends towards the idea that mystics are 'lunatics' deserving confinement, as was written about Blake. I understand the dislike of self-constructed philosophies calculated to promote the egos of clever or foolish people. The doors to heaven and hell are indeed adjacent and identical as one great Greek writer observed. Blake, for example, built on the foundation of Christianity mixed perhaps with Gnosticism, Druidism and Oriental practices. There are well-established, complex doctrines such as Vedanta or Taoism that deserve study before one finds something 'new.' Some do not read, study, listen, learn and may want a quick, happy buzz that sounds interesting. Some will embrace anything shallow that seems exotic ignoring the depths nearby. Likewise, there is also a specifically dark and destructive current of mysticism, which is negative and is associated with black magic and Satanism. That is a real force. Even if you do not believe in it, others do. It is silly however to conclude that all mysticism is bad or vapid.

Critics of mysticism are apt to create definitions to suit their purpose. Fundamentalist Christians seem to use mysticism to refer to something like a Californian New Age sensibility or just pure demonic occultism. Jung denied he was a mystic but many analysts disagree on the basis of the evidence. Philosophers and other writers can be very critical. Bertrand Russell creates an unduly narrow definition and Ayn Rand creates a far wider, unsustainable one. The subject is elusive. Mysticism deals with the 'ineffable' and thus the experience defies words or is indescribable for most, save in relation to identifying some qualities. People also claim they can describe it, but that the description is not it. This links in with ideas about the limit of reason that Kant and Plato dealt with. All higher level things are ultimately abstractions that cannot be imploded by words beyond their essential form into a black hole of meaninglessness. Sufism is the Persian mystical tradition in Islam. One Sufi mystic, many hundreds of years ago, mentioned that knowledge of the conditions of being healthy is not the same as being healthy. Similarly we might think of how difficult it is to explain dreams. Mystical experience is difficult to identify, controversial and always creates opposition. People involved in magic often distinguish it from mysticism, but they overlap at times. Likewise the study of parapsychology may overlap although many consider that a pseudo-science, despite the evidence. The occult will overlap with mysticism in the sense that both deal with the hidden. Nevertheless, mystical experiences create observable effects. We can break it down further to think about mystical experiences or practices and the mystics who engage therewith by chance or choice. It is necessary to try to crystallise the term again. In simple terms, we are talking about a profound inner experience that in effect removes existential despair. However, I would suggest that a fuller definition of mysticism that unites the diverse phenomena in a general way could be the following. Mysticism involves the difficult-to-explain, but meaningful perception or experience of elevated, ecstatic, edifying, extraordinary or altered states of consciousness, involving a loss of self, access to a new reality, combined with a sense of unity and often a distortion of time and space, emerging as a result of practices, or caused by events, which then significantly increase individual commitment to the pursuit of inner wisdom or spiritual consciousness and usually reduce existential despair.

The Nature of Mystical Experience and the Problem of Scientism

There is some evidence that many people claim to have had mystical experiences but also that they will not talk about them. That may be no surprise, for example, if it is about how a plant (such as ayahuasca) has become one's mentor. It is easy to be regarded as insane. If we do not have mystical experiences ourselves then we must rely on reports from others and about others. Such evidence should be assessed like all reports of an equivalent nature. The phenomenon of mystical experience is very well documented. However, there is tension between scientific practice, scientism and the individual. Ironically, while science has often been either dumbfounded or hostile to mysticism, technology has sometimes facilitated it. Eben Alexander is a neuroscientist who had a Near Death Experience (NDE) during an operation and was transported into a new reality that changed his life. His own training told him that nothing should have been happening in his brain at the time it happened. People such as him have communicated eloquently about the realities encountered in extraordinary experiences in altered states. Such events lead people away from specific dogma towards deeper spirituality. This does not mean however that they are going to act inconsistently with the core tenets of religious teaching. In fact, there seems to be a theme in NDEs, about a perception of a sense of justice or karma in the cosmos in these states. There is also a sense of deep individual responsibility that recurs. Technology that keeps people alive means we have more records of such experiences and thus helps in the study of mystical experience. Some academics such as Andrew Newberg and Todd Murphy write about 'neurotheology' and seem to respectfully bridge the science and spirituality chasm. In addition to reports of experience, reliance on mystical and spiritual texts is used to provide evidence of practice and insights also.

Similarly, science may be showing that the suppression of certain mental faculties facilitate these experiences. Thus, for example, concentration in the front of the brain, say through looking at a candle, suppresses the back and the sense of self is temporarily suspended. Brain damage may close down one part that causes another to seek supernatural explanations, some say.

Some think that the brain is a filter and that consciousness is not emergent from the brain. Others will point to temporal lobe epilepsy, psychosis, schizophrenia and seek a pathological explanation of religious experience. There are many studies of religious experience that could be examined. The philosopher and psychologist William James made an effort to study mystical experiences before it became unfashionable to take it seriously. His background made him open to look at the evidence. The phenomenon of people's experience is evidence. Pragmatism as a philosophy, advocates that we look at things from different angles. From a different angle we may glean an angel.

William James studied religious experience as part of his widespread investigations, particularly in his book *The Varieties of Religious Experience,* published at the turn of the twentieth century. James had put psychology on a firm foundation seeking to make it more like a natural science. He admitted that he could not attain any states of mystical consciousness himself but he looked objectively at the evidence. James put mysticism as the root of all religion and I agree with him. He identified four characteristics of mystical states. Firstly, 'ineffability' (meaning inexpressible in words) which sounds negative but really implies that the experiences need to be felt because they are so unusual. Nevertheless, people do explain and describe their experiences and this has been studied scientifically. That may generate the criticism that the experience was not genuinely ineffable and not therefore mystical. This shows the inherent difficulties involved in trying to examine the phenomena. However the quantitative recurrence of words describing mystical experience does not actually tell you much about it. Ineffability really means that language cannot apply to the quality of the experiences itself, because you need knowledge of it as opposed to about it. Secondly 'noetic' which means that they are strangely and authoritatively about increasing knowledge. It is not thinking but some immediate significant feeling which impacts on cognition. Thirdly, less importantly, 'transient,' they are usually short. Fourthly 'passivity' by which he means (I suggest) receptivity characterised by suppression of other stimuli. He looked at states such as sudden realisations and epiphanies, déjà vu, dreamy states, trance and intoxicated states. James thought that these experiences showed that other types of consciousness lay contiguous to our normal, ordinary, rational one. A cosmic consciousness or superconsciousness is perceived. The state is not the key, but rather that state plus the persistent effect of the experience of unity of presence that results from it. 'Samadhi' is the state entered into after proper discipline through practices such as yoga. This can lead to 'Samyama.' Superconsciousness is above reason and ordinary consciousness. Beyond ordinary consciousness is a state, a place. The individual and the Absolute or One come closer together. Object and subject disappear or merge. James, like most sane people, thought that others did not have to accept the revelations as authority but that they did indicate another type of consciousness beyond reason. James focused on the experiences and not the interpretation thereof emphasising the universality, as do other writers such as Underhill. The mystical experience drives the other elements in a religion. Later the other elements take over and people may have no real experience akin to the original sense. I cannot see how awareness of such states threatens anybody.

Since James, there have been a number of important studies. Rudolf Otto developed the concept of the 'numinous.' This was a sense of the divine, which was not rational and not a sensory experience and was still outside the self. It involved profound feelings of awe and mystery. The sense or emotion caused by the holy could not be reduced. Later Stace developed a 'common core' or 'perennialist' approach. Mysticism was defined by an ultimate sense of unity. That unity might be one looking inwards or outwards. It was profound, noetic, blessed, holy, paradoxical and ineffable. Ralph Hood developed a mystical scale that focuses on certain qualities. These were loss of self, unifying sense, inner subjective, time and space becomes changed, noetic, ineffable, positive affect, religious or reverent quality. Hood sees the commonality of the experience at the level of the experience and suggests that only the relating thereof is determined by culture. Hood studied mysticism and came to empirical conclusions that mysticism is common, is not pathological and occurs in all great faith traditions. The intrinsic motivation of mystics in different traditions is still common. Academics such as Katz opposed such commonality across traditions. One big distinction that is relevant to consider is that there is a big split in mysticism, whereby some seem to be aiming for emptiness and some seem to be aiming for fullness. This split can be seen in Taoism and Buddhism for example. There are many academic articles and a lot more interest in recent years. Domains such as Transpersonal Psychology have engaged with the potential and use of altered states of consciousness for psychospiritual development.

Certain scientists, like Sheldrake, use science to study, advance and validate spiritual and mystical practices. That may include meditation, prayer, chanting, fasting or even relating to plants. The key point is that there is a deep dimension of our being, often ignored (unless others can control or use it to control us). Mysticism involves the potential for supreme liberation and that is why mystics recur. That does not mean to say that our mystic faculty cannot be misled or hijacked. Indeed it may be mystics, bright or dark, who know how to do so. The very lack of attention to mysticism may make people prey to gurus, cults and control. It seems that with the development of New Atheism, a degree of hostility to the value of individual experience grew up. The signals seemed to be that science and religion were in a death-battle. This was not true science but 'scientism.' By scientism I mean the ideology that promotes science beyond its proper purpose. Scientism makes science an end and not a means or method. It suggests that science can answer questions that are beyond the limitations of its methods. It makes science the only or dominant source of knowledge even when it is not always appropriate. It makes claims based on scientific authority not justified by the evidence. It extrapolates from natural sciences into social sciences in a cavalier way at times. But science was not always hostile to mysticism. Pythagoras was a highly developed mystic. Einstein demonstrated a mystical technique in the way he approached science as did Newton, Kepler, Edison, Tesla and many others. Many scientific studies came about through dreams, reveries and sudden insights as if from the outside. Descartes was influenced by mystical experience. Einstein put a premium on imagination. People who were both scientific and religious (such as Swedenborg) were mystics. Many mastered the threshold states before and after sleep called the hypnogogic and hypnopompic states.

Now scientists are back. They are grappling with consciousness. They are trying to pin it down. The 'hard problem' of consciousness eludes them. Many believe they will find it and there will be a big demand for the knowledge they acquire. The origin and nature of consciousness is the holy grail. The results of scientific studies about consciousness are often depressing efforts in reductionism and tell us more about scientific consciousness. When they cannot find it they say it does not exist. There are others in the domains of neuroscience and neurotheology who seem more respectful. Some have developed concepts such as self-transcendent experiences (STEs) to describe states involving loss of a sense of self and boundaries with an increased feeling of connectedness. Your boundaries will dissolve and that allows some new sense of relation. This would be wider than mystical experiences, but include them. Mystical experience however seems to be characterised by being more memorable and significant. A zig-zagging between the two brain hemispheres is another explanation. One key development recently seems to be that writers are seeing a general mystical zone instead of separate fields.

Pim van Lommel made a celebrated prospective and longtitudinal study of experiences of people who experienced cardiac arrest and clinical death and who should not have any consciousness but did. No breathing, no circulation but enhanced consciousness was consistently reported and recorded by medical personnel. It contradicted the standard material explanation. The enhanced, non-local consciousness has self-identity, memories, emotions and cognition. It is believed to be a reality and not an illusion and affects the experiencer significantly. Similarly, Bruce Greyson made prospective studies and questioned the idea of the location of consciousness in the brain, if the sensorium and complex cognition exists during near death experiences. Out-of-body experiences, life review, deceased relatives and an experience of simultaneousness and instant entanglement with others and being able to follow your thoughts are well recorded. It strikes me that such work shows that the enhanced consciousness is indeed beyond the senses at some point. It may be that the spiritual consciousness accesses a different dimension. It is non-local consciousness and time and space disappear. Dr Kenneth Ring compared NDE's with UFO's experiences and found a remarkable pattern of similarity in the effects thereof in his book *The Omega Project: Near Death Experiences, UFO's and Mind at Large*. More recently there have been books such as *Beyond UFOS: The Science of Consciousness and Contact with Non-Human Intelligence*. This relates to ideas such as Quantum Holograms.

It is interesting that William James influenced Walter Evans-Wentz when the latter was a student. Evans-Wentz later went on to translate the *Tibetan Book of The Dead*. Parallels between the experiences outlined therein and NDE's have been noted. Timothy Leary used this book as the basis for *The Psychedelic Experience* in relation to dealing with 'ego death' under the influence of hallucinogenic drugs. Evans-Wentz did his PhD at Oxford on The Fairy Faith in Celtic Countries. The descriptions of beings he recorded as a 'gypsy scholar' therefor, parallel the more recent studies of interactions between people and non-human intelligences, often in a UFO context. I believe that mysticism may be the trunk of this tree with many branches and not merely a branch itself.

Some scientists seem sympathetic to spirituality and argue that you should engage in these practices because they are good for you. They may open you up and help lead to a well-ordered life. However if you say that drugs and adventure sports are all 'spiritual' experiences, without any other value or notion, then we are dealing with something else. A sense of 'Oneness' that comes about jumping off a cliff may be very significant but it does not offer a spiritual system. Compassion towards oneself and others is a sign of a proper path for example. That is not a political ideology however. Mental toughness, discipline and coherence may be others. A buzz is not an answer to the great bewildering that seeks resolving. The mystical experience is a current that gets deeper if one goes with the flow. At some stage we must reflect on our own spiritual consciousness. When we reflect on our own consciousness, we get drawn into consideration of a deeper notion. Max Planck thought that consciousness was fundamental in the universe. Mysticism is a key. Mystics, whatever their beliefs, were explorers in consciousness, perhaps voyagers in a different dimension. Mystical experience is part of a triangle with spirit and consciousness as the other angles. Many scientists are using technology to try pin mystical states and spirituality down in the brain in a reductive way. Many will seek to take out the spirit in the end. They will banish the ghost from the machine. However there are some scientists who now say that the mystical faculty is real and has evolved to be useful for our survival.

What are mystics? What do they do? Who are they?

Based on the number of definitions above, it is clear that a wide range of activity makes many mystics. By mystic here I mean people who engage in mystical practices or experiences in some committed way. Mystics must be in some persistent pursuit of the level of experience they may experience once. If they do not like it, they will leave it. Other things may be more meaningful for them and perhaps others. Mystics are motivated by intrinsic, inner reasons. It is important to state that there are mystics who are religious and spiritual, some who are just spiritual and even some who are neither religious or spiritual. There seems to be recurrent, common elements or patterns, if we look at the perspective of those who engage in mysticism. In that sense I suppose I would be classified as a 'perennialist.' Perennial philosophy says that similar spiritual insight and experiences exist everywhere. Some argue for a perennial psychology as a result. This perspective carries the idea of a 'common core' or 'unity thesis' that there is a unity of mystical experiences across cultures in studies. This is opposed to the view that focuses on 'constructivist' or 'diversity' theory. That is academic but may be indicative. If you are in a bus station, look at the destination of the bus before you get on it. Mystical traditions bring you to different places. I am arguing more in that perennial mode and I do see the centre being in the spirit. I am sceptical of mysticism on its own without recognising the spirit. Mystical experiences for people who have no religious or spiritual life should at least establish a chain of comprehension if not of exploration. Seriously mature spiritual practitioners (such as the Tibetan Buddhists) often recommend to stick to the system you are most familiar with and go deeper. As they say, don't ignore the elephant beside you, to go looking for elephant footprints in the forest. Still, the path of mystical experience calls all who are so inclined. There is a new tendency to separate all mysticism from 'dogma' to get the benefits of well-being in a psychological sense. I believe this is reductionist and spirit-denying although very useful. We should find our spiritual splendour before pale substitutes.

Mystics may enter trances, contemplate, meditate, dance, pray, chant, fast, retreat, wander, work, paint, make or write. So, what a person does may be part of it. However, those activities are never an end for the mystic but a way to the higher. It may be obvious that a certain person is spiritual. Alternatively, there may be no garlands, bells, gowns or outward sign of religious or spiritual activity. We think we know what others might think but we know so little. The inner world is secret and save for the reports of those who explore it, we would know less. Mystics often do not articulate their experiences, particularly in a climate of severe scepticism. People who have had Near Death Experiences are often silent about it because it is ineffable, it is felt and it affects them permanently. Such people often did not want to come back and found it difficult to re-adjust despite the lack of fear of death. Maslow indicated how hard it was to get actualised people to talk and feed into scientific study. I think their reluctance is good and demonstrates an intuition that there is a sense that scientific method will suck out what it wants while scientism undermines what is not capable of reduction.

So genuine mystics will more consistently engage deeply with the inner life and employ practices to go deeper and climb higher. We might say there is some mystic commitment or potential. But a sole mystical event may cause such commitment. Mystics, or the people involved in mystical activities, are willing to explore and engage with extrasensory, supernatural and hidden forces. Mystics discover or seek deep meaning above all. They develop an antenna of meaning. Why people make a mystic commitment may depend on diverse reasons from natural disposition to chance and circumstance. Mystical experience may come out of the blue for certain people. A single extraordinary encounter may affect the entire existence of the experiencer thereafter according to the evidence. Mysticism may be fundamentally practical. The Shaman went into an altered state of consciousness often to find answers to improve survival chances for the group. It is often thus about survival rather than selfish, subjective escapism. Mystics may come to strange conclusions, sometimes counter-intuitively. They may value intuitions, inclinations or senses. Mystics are commonly associated with the founders of religions. Mystics will place their experience higher than some external rules. Mystics engage with what is incomprehensible and inaccessible to other forms of knowledge. They are deeply subjective, idealist and individualistic. Mystics may claim to see or engage with other beings. Unsurprisingly such people are easily characterised as mad. Mysticism may lead to God or the Devil, heaven or hell, as it overlaps with religion and magic. Mysticism is closely associated with creativity and imagination in both art and science. Mystics value meaning of a type that corresponds with their mystical life. More generally, it is often conceived in terms of finding the light inside and re-connecting with the eternal light. The mystic commitment affects the worldview, actions and behaviour of the mystic seeker.

Who are the mystics? Scholars have made us aware of certain influential mystics. Thus in Catholicism, or early Christianity, they point to Origen and Clement of Alexandria and early monasticism. There were also many early Christian, mystical traditions suppressed by the Church. The Gnostics might be mentioned and on the Jewish side the Essenes or Therapeutae. The Celtic Church was distinctive and reflected some pre-Christian spirituality. Before it was ousted, it had established a unique spirituality which revered nature, created beautiful illuminated scripts, spiritual hermits and wandering teachers. In the 1200's in Christianity there was a shift that led to what was known as the New Mysticism. This entailed a moving of mysticism from the elite to the mass of people. A similar thing happened with Taoism during the Song dynasty in China. That gave access in plainer language to more people, away from the enclosures and attracted more women. This was linked sometimes to erotic descriptions of divine ecstasy. An accessible doctrine of practice which encouraged rapture and divine seeking, without the structures of the Church, obviously posed a threat to people who wanted authority and control. This led to the 'Free Spirits' which was a heresy for the faithful. That brand of religion was more individual and based on an idea of the significance of spirit and the Holy Spirit in particular. Any study of Martin Luther shows the deep debt to mysticism, experience and study that formed the basis of Protestant doctrine. The Quakers later would most represent the immediacy and primary nature of the mystical path. Figures such as Jacob Boehme stand out in the Protestant world. English Protestants poets and Puritans were also interested in mysticism. The reaction to the Reformation involved another infusion of mysticism. In Judaism there are a number of schools of mysticism including Kabbalah and Merkabah. Such doctrines were generally for the elite and learned.

Mysticism was mostly for elites but broke out at stages for the masses. Thus there has long been an argument that anyone can be or should be engaged in or aware of mysticism. Many people do not seem, however, disposed to mysticism. I suspect that there are more serious mystics who do not talk about their mystical experience than pseudo-mystics who prattle on about it. Remember, however, that for most of human history people lived in an enchanted world where the mystical was the norm. Some assert that the followers of the monotheistic religions report less mystical experiences. This is probably because religion has mysticism embedded into ritual. Mystics first reveal and then legalists, the Scribes and the Pharisees, take over. Then the people who ask you to accept the mystic world that once existed will vehemently deny any persistence of it today. The teachings and practices of mystics may be forced underground, literally. But many spiritual traditions revere mystics and use their insights to infuse stale dogma with new life. It is strange however that 'objectivists' like Ayn Rand claim that all religion is mysticism. She goes further and weirdly attributes Communism to mysticism despite its unavoidably materialist essence. In Christianity, the Catholic Church tended to want to bring mysticism out and require that it was not closed and secret as the earlier Greeks arguably emphasised. That was usually after some persistence of examination and evidence. However much was left out and after the Reformation many streams were diverted.

People may spend a lifetime studying esoteric things and engaging in mysticism intellectually or actually. Famous figures including Rudolf Steiner, Manly P. Hall, Aldous Huxley, Crowley, Osho and Gurdjieff come to mind. Esoteric philosophy underlies the work of Mozart and Beethoven. Writers often have critical mystical experiences. Philip K. Dick was one who focused on Science Fiction and whose novels lay behind popular films such as *Blade Runner*, *Total Recall* and *Minority Report*. He was preoccupied with one mystical experience whereby he believed that Logos, or some divine force which he called 'VALIS,' communicated information and knowledge instantaneously in a beam of light on 2-3-74. If you read *The Exegesis of Philip K. Dick* (which is getting on to one thousand pages from 8000 pages) that Dick wrote after his experience, you see how profound and utterly bewildering the effect of a mystical experience may be. That process of 'anamnesis' links back to Plato and the idea that we have, inside us, access to our past and the experience of divine company before we came here. The soul is fixed on the body and pleasure, pain and the trauma of being born into it make us forget. Alternatively we drink a draught of forgetfulness before we come in. Nevertheless it lies there for us to re-acquaint ourselves with. But the spiritual vehicles go to different places. Manly Hall came to some of the same insights I do but then draws a significantly different conclusion. Consciousness is pre-existent and persistent he agrees. But he concludes that no God could condemn someone for evil because it would only be ignorance that disappears in the arc of time. I do not think this is what spiritual leaders were saying.

Much occurs underground and behind closed doors. Remember that historians cannot tell us much about secret societies. Some biographies only make sense when you factor in membership of a secret club. Parapsychology overlaps at times with mysticism. People who practice 'remote-viewing' and the like may be involved in mysticism, but not necessarily. Some believe that such pursuits are merely developments of inherent human power while others believe that such investigations are demonic. The US defence forces have employed such practitioners at times. The practice of magic and alchemy may overlap with the mystical journey but are often clearly distinguished. John Dee, the original 007, was a magician for Queen Elizabeth as well as a mystic and a man of science. Mystics come to reject the exclusivity of material and mechanistic explanations. They reject the dominance of materialism and the worship of the machine and matter.

Physical activity involving 'inspiration' may refer to a mystical process. Movement, dance, yoga or martial arts may involve mystical elements. Capoeira has the form of an obvious mystical practice. Many leaders were mystics. Our physical health is part of our whole health and our spiritual health is intimately connected. When photographs of Thich Quang Duc's self-immolation in Vietnam in 1963 went around the world it was striking how serene he was. His self-control was of the nature of someone who has mastered their body and mind. Mystics often learn to subjugate the normal actions of their body. Mystical and spiritual practices can enhance mind and body health. There is a similar trend in the work of some contemporaries like Wim Hof, who seek control of the physical body and mind. Breath, spirit, consciousness and body have always been linked in the spiritual quest. Hof looks at other senses and neurological networks such as the sixth sense, proprioception and nociception. If we add magnetoception and equilibrioception we can question some of the assumptions made by philosophers with a limited idea of senses. This links into Tummo, the Inner Fire in Tibetan Buddhism. The mystics may be demonstrating higher levels of control over the physical body and we can all benefit from that. Thus many physical practices may have mystical connections. Even the proponents of theories that suggest we live in some type of computer simulation may further suggest that such a theory would allow contact with the creator or managers of that world.

So, mystics often see the world differently. They are more at peace, less egotistical, less materialistic and less concerned about some normal things. They will reject elements of the orthodoxy if necessary. Their literal insight and vision make them march to the beat of a distant drum. They will be willing to be alone, a maverick, a voice in the wilderness. That is consistent with the view of the hermit in the cave, although in Plato's story we had to leave the cave of projections. The evidence shows that mystics often come back from isolation. That isolation may even be more of a mental nature amongst millions of people. They come back with views and visions. They are the prophets. They come back with talents and tales. They often put it into words. They then act. They may establish organisations, orders. They may dis-establish the existing order. With a certainty of self they can compel others who have none. Charisma is a special favour or grace that comes from inside but whose nature is from the beyond. The innovators, the inventors, the creators, the disturbers, the charismatic leaders will have some inner power. That power comes from an exile, journey and alienation. In that absence the world becomes clearer. Ayn Rand seemed to think that the first movers were always self-interested rationalists motivated by material gain. That is too simplistic. It is true that mystics may ignore the material more than they should because the spiritual world triumphs over it for them. But when the material world threatens the spiritual one, they will eventually engage.

Mysticism is universal in the present and past. Angels are everywhere and many people readily accept these. Mysticism is at the base of much of the contemporary Law of Attraction, which in turn came from the New Thought movement which was from a Christian base at some stages. Esther and Jerry Hicks claim to channel a group of non-physical entities or intelligences called 'Abraham.' Similarly the New Age movement was encouraged by *The Seth Material* which were words supposedly coming from 'Seth,' an entity from beyond. Similarly the book *A Course in Miracles* claims to be channelled. These works are clearly popular, so the reality of their influence and claims cannot be ignored even if one thinks them demonic. In the past we see mysticism underlying Taoism, for example. The Lakota Sioux look to Watan Tanka which is the 'Great Mystery.' Shamanism is an essentially mystical endeavour. Toltec shamanism has come to wider attention recently with other forms. Most shamans do not use psychedelic substances and generally use standard techniques of repetitive drumming, movement, spinning and so on. Shamanism underlines the point that individual experience has been transmuted into group experience. That does not mean that everyone can do it. There are often, therefore, elite groups of people who must train to be mystics if they are not naturally so disposed. There is an important general issue here. Not everyone can or should engage in mystical practices even if they are disposed thereto. It does not suit some and can be positively destructive for people. That may explain why there may have been often a degree of elitism and control in relation to mystical practices. Initiation was most likely first a filter mechanism. In addition, knowledge is power and many may have been involved in mystical sects for control of others. In the past and present, many women mystics have had a huge influence. Helen Keller was influenced by Swedenborg and developed her own unique contribution through action and example. Edith Stein was another not to forget. We see mysticism also in the Transcendentalists like Thoreau and Whitman. As mentioned above, neuroscience and the ability to resuscitate people have given rise to a body of scientific information about Near Death Experiences. Some people also have medical conditions that may contribute to more of such experiences. There is no doubt that people in the past who had such experiences had their perceptions changed. That scientism says we must crawl as if to Caesar to prove it, even when such proof emanates from its own tools, shows how hostile its inner tendency has become. Scientism wants science for other purposes it seems. The forces of disenchantment will sacrifice meaning on the altar of progress.

Mystics as Leaders

All the great religious leaders were mystics or behaved like mystics. Within Christianity, for example, we see St Francis, St John of the Cross, Ignatius of Loyola, Julian of Norwich, Teresa of Avila, Boehme, Hildegard of Bingen, Birgitta of Sweden. This is a very specific, disciplined, well-studied phenomenon about individuals connecting to God or Jesus back to the early Church and monks in particular. The connection for Christian mystics involves an ecstatic, revelatory or comforting, unmediated experience combined with an enhanced sense of direct and divine presence that leads to some kind of knowledge or knowing that is personally transforming. Christian mystics point to a separation, withdrawal, subtraction, reduction or, on the contrary, a perception of all-pervasive divinity. It may be a journey to nothingness that sounds like Oriental philosophy or theology and thus, paradoxically, beyond all phenomena or a sense of immersion in a unitive cosmos. Mystics usually then accomplish things and often reform.

Mahatma Gandhi was a true mystic who discovered the path and with his 'silent inward revolution' came back with a way to assist people. Martin Luther King was a Christian with a deep mystical background who had studied the mystery religions. Mystical leaders often behave differently, sound prophetic, act inspired. History is littered with anomalous individuals who were mystics. There are three I would mention to give a flavour. Christian mystics abound, some accepted and some rejected. Joan of Arc was one of the most amazing. The history is well recorded about a girl who becomes a military leader to save France but is eventually burned at the stake by the Church. Rasputin is another. History is being rewritten about the 'mad monk,' who probably did not do many of the bad things attributed to him. He may have been more vilified because he opposed oppression of the Russian Jews and he was against war. His healing powers were another feature associated with mystical people. Edgar Cayce 'the sleeping prophet' is an example of a clairvoyant who attained fame for healing people in a trance without medical training. Many Christians would claim he was not a Christian. As well as individuals there are also mystical groups. The Cathars are another group of Christians destroyed because of their more mystical mutations of doctrine. What a person believes may be a matter of life or death. Islam and Judaism likewise have a long tradition of mysticism.

Very few great artists were not mystics. William Blake was one of the greatest. Da Vinci, Michelangelo, Van Gogh and so on come to mind. Some (such as Jonathan Black in *The Secret History of the World*) have argued that they were driven by a secret and esoteric philosophy of the spirit. Similar arguments have been advanced more notably by Manly Hall in *The Secret History of all the Ages*. However Van Gogh was a deeply spiritual man without any commitment to a group after he left the Church. Mystical processes of inspiration could be suggested about many who were not mystical at all. Francis Bacon, the atheist painter talked about how the images came into his head unbidden. Many writers, such as Dickens, conceived their novels in a hypnogogic or hypnopompic state before they fell asleep or woke up. Many writers talk about the core of novels coming as if from outside. Mary Poppins is one example. P.L. Travers was much into mysticism. Strindberg was heavily involved in alchemy, magical and mystical pursuits. Tolstoy developed into a mystic partly through his intellectual searching. He has a realisation and later elaborated theories of non-violence that would influence Gandhi and Martin Luther King. His religious faith came in a sudden insight and developed through communication with groups like the Quakers. The poetic muses or 'daemons' have been around for a long time. In many books and films we see the mystic insights applied. The Matrix reflects Gnostic debates about the nature of reality. Mystical experiences have consequences.

Dark, Destructive, Negative Mysticism

'Dark' mysticism is an adjective I am using here in the simple sense of the absence of light, with my indication that the type I refer to is dangerous. Within mysticism there is 'antinomian' mysticism, which goes against the established rules, such as for example, that associated with Anne Hutchinson (1591-1643). To some extent much mysticism is antinomian, it depends on the precise definition. The term had a very specific meaning in Christianity and made reference to whether you could be saved by works or grace. But it seems to be used also to describe groups such as the Aghora in India who break taboos and utilise transgressions to shock in order to come to the highest.

Similarly, there have always been groups such as the Carpocratians who thought paradoxically that appeasing Satan was a path to God. Some of the practices of old are conjecture and some of the present are sensational. I would be sympathetic to Anne Hutchinson and even Rasputin while some other practices are not my cup of tea and not everything can be supported because it is seen to be mystical or spiritual. If you chose to do damage to yourself (which I am not in favour of) that is ultimately up to you. I see that some use the term 'dark mysticism' to refer to a mysticism of nature without God, a pantheism and I do not mean it so. Some use it to refer to the dark grandeur of nature. I am using 'dark' to indicate something negative because of the absence of light. There is a problem in that many mystics talk of the 'dazzling darkness,' the need to embrace the dark, the need to retreat into the dark in order to experience solitude and silence. It is not that but the destructive effects of certain mysticism that I refer to here. A pragmatic view makes you look at what people do and what effects they have, in order to assess what it is they are about.

Unfortunately, Hitler might be mystical and his nemesis Churchill also had mystical tendencies. If Hitler was not a mystic (which I think he was) he was certainly very influenced by mystics. Churchill's writings refer to 'providence' and his good luck as well as deep intimations throughout his writings and his associations with esoteric organisations is known. In recent generations, war has been launched on a basis which purports to be mystical at times. On the dark mystical side, there is also the phenomenon or reality of demonic possession. This is taken seriously in religious traditions and others. The attempt to engage with spirits and beings is a dangerous one. If a person seeks to engage with demons then arguably we have a type of dark mysticism. If a person has sought such things then they engage knowingly or unknowingly therewith. They may have got on a dark path or wandered carelessly there. If one is sceptical or scientific to such a degree that one can never accept that a person can be affected adversely by attempted engagement with destructive entities then perhaps one can admit that people on a dark path may gain intellectual momentum from doctrines that act on their mind through dabbling therein. Empathy is not just a nice feeling in a pleasant context about your best friend, dog or relation. It also requires an engagement in trying to understand that with which you have no identification. If human behaviour is rule-governed, then we should look to the rules people operate by and not how we think they ought to behave on the basis of our lazy projections onto them. The modest attempt here to indicate the reality of the path of the spirit does not compel the vehicle therefor. However, it is clear that there is a positive, good direction indicated by values of enlightenment, compassion, empathy and love. In Biblical terms one could refer to Galatians 5. 22-23. *"But the fruits of the spirit is love, joy, peace, forbearance, kindness, goodness, faithfulness, gentleness and self-control."* Buddhist scriptures emphasise similar qualities. It is a spiral whereby the values manifested and pursued become magnified.

Mysticism is therefore not necessarily good and has this negative side. Himmler was another driven by a dark mysticism. If you think mysticism is nonsense then you cannot understand the way our world works. If we ignore the creativity or destructiveness that emanates from the lonely mind, then we do so at our peril and own loss. Aleister Crowley was clearly a mystic and seen as very wicked by many, although much more accepted now. People who open themselves up to the hidden and the occult are engaging in dangerous practices from a psychological perspective. You may not believe it, but I believe that the phenomenon of possession and madness can be associated with such activities. Satanism, which covers a whole spectrum from the mild to the destructive, is mystical though it promotes materialism. The link between music and the sale of the soul to the devil reflects some kind of truth. Swedenborg, the great mystic, wrote that much mental disorder was caused by possession by spirits. This was followed up by the psychologist Wilson van Dusen in his work. Whether one accepts that or not, it is important not to mess around with the mind and unleash the unknown.

Religions and cults can be established by charlatans and con-men and women to exploit and control. Sceptics properly emphasise the need to examine supernatural claims and individuals with apparent powers. Mind control techniques often involve some kind of mystical intervention through hallucinogens and psychoactive drugs. I am suspicious about drugs that induce mystical experience and there are very practical dangers not least illegality, exploitation and abuse. I think the short cut is dangerous for many. I know it may work for some but the other work has to be done. I have no doubt that these substances, which are part of traditional environmental knowledge, create what are mystical experiences. In certain cases it may help and there is a growing body of evidence to support the healing potential of such plants. Advocates say there is evidence about the positive impact on depression particularly for treatment resistant depression for example. DMT is the psychedelic component of ayahuasca which was seen to be a medicine. However psychosis and other mental problems may be risks to some. The beneficial reports are suggested to be about rejecting addiction and being more compassionate and authentic towards oneself, according to writers such as Rachel Harris. Those results or realisation of compassion should be general objectives in all positive spiritual paths. A temporary experience still needs to be integrated into behaviour in life. Similarly peyote, psilocybin and LSD have been regarded as 'entheogens' aimed at spiritual development. The word entheogen is from the Greek, meaning to be full of god, and is the root of the word 'enthusiasm.' Mushrooms have long been used in many cultures. However, when such drugs or derivatives are being promoted by the State or commercial interests, one has to be careful. Mind control facilitated by the ruling class or government is dangerous. Coca leaves in an indigenous community are not the same as cocaine in an urban environment. Indigenous communities have knowledge of plants that is real, powerful and useful. Huxley is seen as a liberating influence in this domain but he can, equally, be considered part of the establishment promoting a completely different agenda. Indigenous knowledge and associated spiritual practices should be propagated principally by them. Huxley died on the same day as C.S. Lewis. Lewis came to Christianity through a combined intellectual and mystical way. They both died on the same day as Kennedy. I think time will show Lewis to have made the greater contribution to genuine spiritual development. Finally I find it slightly difficult to accept that some people from the West who have had no real spiritual life (by their own reports) will gladly cede spiritual authority to a plant spirit without any knowledge of spiritual discernment. Spirits cause madness according to certain mystics. Nevertheless, I support the right of people on spiritual journeys to engage in their explorations. The evidence from Timothy Leary and onwards to Roland Griffiths and others suggested that psychedelically induced mystical states may create similar, direct effects as other mystical approaches. It was suggested that such drugs might help prisoners stop committing crime. They help people stop smoking. However, it is clear that absent a system of support, the drugs will not have long-term spiritual effects. Huston Smith who wrote *The World's Religions*, suggested that drug-induced experiences do not necessarily create the same effects for the community as other paths. My guess is that a mystical experience is only a platform and the quality of subsequent experience will be determined by commitment thereafter. I suspect that a short cut may miss the sources of fuel that ultimately give momentum in the long run. You may get the sugar and not the whole fruit.

There are also mystical experiences which allow access to superconsciousness but which prove to be negative. William James refers to the Vedantists who say that if you just stumble into superconsciousness then the results will be impure. This is the same as Christians warning about demons and devils. This is the same as psychologists warning about the negative effects of intoxicants for mental health. Some in the BDSM community argue that there is a mystical element to what they do. That may be true but absent any attempt to direct spiritual evolution it is a different endeavour. There is no doubt that the language of submission, goddesses and so on makes a direct reference to the same domain as mysticism and it may seek to be a substitute. The simple point emerges. All genuine, positive or right mysticism is based on some fundamental principles that may be seen to be consistent with universal principles or the universal moral law for some. This split between bright and dark mysticism, good and bad, reflects splits between the right-handed path and the left-handed path in magic. The mysticism may come by chance or discipline and put a person on the right path. The powers that come from higher levels are not the object of the search but the consequence and they are to be largely ignored as a by-product of a deeper mission. The suggestion is that the purity of heart, compassion and mastery of the body and mind are universal signposts. Magic may be the Western concentration on the 'siddhis' or psychic gifts that are known in the East to come from spiritual practice. There is also a lot of evidence to suggest that esoteric secret societies want to promote spiritual, mystical or esoteric practices as a 'science' to promote a proper order. Such an approach has to be negative.

Anti-Mystics. Opposition to Mysticism

Why do some have a problem with mysticism or mystics and why do people oppose it? We can learn by looking at who opposes mysticism. I mentioned destructive mysticism above. If we are talking about dark mysticism, then many other mystics will oppose it. By their fruits you will know them. The use and inversion of practices to achieve nefarious goals is clearly the opposite of the good path. People will often tell you there is no good or right path and you can believe them at you own peril. However people also have a right to explore and develop their own consciousness, which needs to be respected and not everything from a pre-historical source is negative as some believe. As we have seen, the first tactic is to create an unduly wide or narrow definition of mysticism or utilise a secondary meaning thereof. That is usually then juxtaposed against the doctrine the proponents of such definitions seek to promote. Thus the main opponents of mysticism, the principal anti-mystics, are fundamentalist or extreme scientists, atheists, objectivists and established religious 'authorities.' As I have indicated, scientists can be hostile to mysticism. The problem is that scientific method is fantastic for many things, but fails when we deal with first causes. Since the Enlightenment, consciousness has been reduced. Science will not tell you what happens before the Big Bang and where that came from. It will not tell you where consciousness came from or even where it resides. It finds that certain things are just anomalies or oddities even if they are recorded for millennia. It will certainly not deal with meaning or the really important questions and when it does it tends towards the most unsatisfactory ends. It is not neutral. If scientists cannot measure it and mystics are not always participating in those things and they do not value it, there is no surprise that the mindsets do not meet. Mystics seek to rise above the thinking mind at critical times, not to deny its value but to add to it. New Atheism has opposed much although it is changing its approach slightly. At the same time, Quantum Theory shows us that the world is stranger than we can imagine.

The scientific mindset allies with certain associated philosophical positions. Ayn Rand is one of the greatest opponents of mysticism. She was an 'objectivist.' She put 'reason' and rational self-interest as the highest values and hated mysticism. Reality was independent of consciousness. The problem is that her definition of mysticism was so wide as to include all of religion. Her use of the term makes it meaningless. However, I accept her basic objection that mysticism stops the selfish self-realisation she prizes. I would object that her curious individualism stops people exploring their individuality. While I agree with her on the role of the State, I find that her disregard of institutions is strange. She seems more like a tyrant in disposition, to me. Her opposition to 'sacrifice' would ensure that we cannot defend ourselves against the tyranny she claimed to oppose. I have no doubt that she would have a problem with self-sacrifice but be less concerned with the sacrifice of others. But she is right that whatever someone comes back with from the cave or their reverie may not be easily transferable. You can see it where certain Zen and Yoga writers give you their discipline as techniques with the spirit and mysticism squeezed out. However, one important point made by people who have studied mystics is that they bring something tangible back through their message or actions. Often the action implements the feeling and speaks louder than words. The dismissal of mystics as inarticulate babblers with untestable insights removed from reality is false in relation to the committed mystic.

Well-established religions often oppose mystics or may make it hard for them. It depends on the mystic and their activity. They may want to threaten the foundations of the established religion but more often they may just want a new skylight or to water the plants that are sheltered therein. Martin Luther was a mystic. Evangelical Christians, some Catholics and others today oppose mysticism. They see it as a dangerous departure from orthodoxy and scripture that may be heresy, apostasy or Satanic. This is a serious objection. I would argue that we must start off by developing our knowledge, intellectual and critical faculties as much as possible. That is a lifelong pursuit. To do that, we must wake up from the hypnotic trance that western society has framed for us. If you are religious you follow the rules. Certain sects such as the Quakers operate on the basis of direct mystical experience. The individual is inspired and then communicates it to the community. However religious practice should promote spiritual development. If the external practice does not transfer to the interior it cannot amount to anything. The exterior must influence the interior and then the internal may be externalised. The worship of words and

34

rules is not what spiritual activity is about. External spiritual truths need a tilled field. There must be growth. Some Christians cite St Paul, although his conversion involves a mystical experience. But we are at a basic level. The very existence of the idea of individual spirit and consciousness is under attack. There will be no tilled field to plant anything. Is Christianity going to throw out all the Christian mystics because it does not like mysticism? Vectors of general spirituality are not the same as specific vectors of dogma. At the same time churches have become more involved in political struggles about material welfare.

The notion of the 'Hero's Journey' is associated with Campbell and underlies many thinkers from George Lucas to Jordan Peterson. I believe this is a description of the path of spiritual evolution rather than a mere pattern for existential meaning. Each individual needs to be a hero. This is the archetypal story that Jung and others mention. The hero goes off on their journey but they bring something back. The true mark of the mystic comes in what they say, do or contribute. In Christianity, science, art and leadership mystics contribute all the time. They do not overthrow reason, they add to it through visions. There is a danger that many religions or power structures become the province of the legalists, literalists, Scribes or the Pharisees. The mystic may be dangerous to orthodoxy. They may be the revolutionaries or counter-revolutionaries. Many mystics go away, retreat then realise and return. The Taoists retreated to the mountains. The Transcendentalists retreated somewhat and cultivated civil disobedience. Evelyn Underhill emphasised how mystics bring something back and do things in the world.

Certain individuals hate mysticism and you can almost see it in their eyes. Sometimes because they hate the spirit that cannot be controlled, sometimes it is because their mode of being leaves them out, sometimes because they have been programmed with scientism and atheism or antitheism. Ideological anti-mysticism may use arguments and objections that have some validity. Mysticism of a genuine and elevated nature creates hostility in those who see that it opposes their agenda. But there are some pseudo-mystics who promote distrust. There are many who wish to pretend that their experience is unique. Mesmerism can be used to exploit other people. Cults can use mystical practice as a fundamental part of their arsenal.

In every walk of life there are frauds and charlatans. Mysticism is a complement to reason and rationality. Mysticism may be the yin to the yang. Nevertheless mysticism is no excuse to avoid rationality or reason. Mysticism is no excuse for ignorance. Indeed the failure to understand the world, the institutions, known and unknown represents a threat to the whole and thus everything that involves mysticism. We should recognise that we walk on land and swim in water when we move between reason and revelation.

Reasonable Mysticism. Reconciling Tensions

We can deal with mysticism from the standpoint of epistemology and ontology. Some say that the subjective ontology can become objective epistemology. We could use the concept of the whole of knowledge or holistic knowledge to bring them together. These are the building blocks of the philosophy of knowing. Philosophy and science often dismiss individual claims because they are not testable and measurable. There are more subtle problems. For example, Abraham Maslow was frustrated when studying peak experiences because people who reach high levels are often unwilling to engage in scientific studies. The self-actualised person who has reached the heights of human endeavour, and probably has more of a plateau of experience, is not going to value the attempt to pin it down. A person who is an Idealist or relies on subjective experience may also argue that epistemology is a construct, not existing in the real world. 'Idealism' as a philosophy tends towards the spiritual and against external material reality. There are so many debates about objective v. subjective, epistemology v. ontology and dualism v. monism that it can paralyse the person. Let the philosophers chew on those issues like dogs on a bone. Many philosophers are propagandists and the taxonomy and compartments they frown about are never the thing itself.

I think it is easy to reconcile the tensions. The mystic is engaged in direct experience which impacts primarily on them. That is subjective. That subjectivity is transformable into objective knowledge or information. It may be a difficult process. Already 'phenomenological' approaches mean that you can listen to explanation or reports of experience and extract knowledge or information therefrom. That means that people can study what the mystics say or do and assess it.

There may be paradox in that the phenomenology leads to thinking about something above phenomena. Even if you reach a satisfactory reconciliation you will met the deeper thinking that says that there can be no subject and no object. Mind and reality are inherently linked. Buddhism often breaks down some of these illusions. Distinctions can help but the danger is that when arguing about details we mistake them for the thing itself. Either/or, is a trap at times.

Mysticism is complementary to 'reason.' Reason was defined generally by sense perception. Mysticism is a sense of the spirit capable of being developed. It may be that claims to universal moral laws or divine justice or karma is of this domain. It may be that conscience, the essence of individual morality, is an informed instinct, a sense of justice. However in order to control the mystic faculty, science and psychology are both engaging with it. The obvious intellectual fundamentalism underneath the cloak of reason of the New Atheists may have been partially counter-productive, so that some seek to infiltrate instead. Alternatively, the obvious success of the scorched earth policy of strident scientism for one generation may have encouraged them to complete the cultural revolution they want. On the other side there are movements such as 'Interspirituality' which seek to function through examining the common core. New terms emerge but I do not find them always helpful. For example Persistent Non-Symbolic Experience (PSNE) is used to refer to non-dual awareness, enlightenment, mystical, peak and also transcendental experience, union with God and the peace that passeth understanding. There is a benefit from learning from others and practices are enhanced in groups but I think the mystical path must have many solitary steps. One trend is to extract the method of mysticism from cross-cultural sources, strip dogma away and use the proven methods for psychological well-being. This moves away from spirituality all together. This is not my way. That does not mean that insights such as the different levels or 'locations' of experience are not valuable, admirable or useful. Likewise, the pursuit of 'Oneness' through purely physical means gives great peace to many but it is not the end for me. There is a danger of the ship of commercial science, blown with the winds of scientism, plundering the bounty of spiritual practice and scuttling the source thereof.

The Need for Awareness of Power and Value of Mysticism

Here is why I believe my poetic attempt to deal with mysticism is important. Firstly, people need to connect to a deeper meaning. Much of what purports to deal with such things are pale substitutes or propaganda. We need to get a sense of who we are and actively tend to that field or garden. We need to create a sense of our inner power. This is not just crucial for ourselves but has wider implications. I believe that there is a war of the spirit going on in the western world. On one side is science and the dangerous offspring it should take responsibility for, namely scientism. The techniques and methods of science claim exclusivity since the Enlightenment. They mow down opposing forces of religion and spirituality. They seem to relish their disenchanting role. Much has been lost ever since. Christianity is being supplanted. I see a deeper existential threat. Scientists, collectivists, materialists have allied to create a technocratic oligarchy where technology and the machine rule. This may link to clandestine political agendas. There has been a war on spiritual belief. One prong is to ridicule, attack, undermine and boycott it. Dawkins is an example of that fundamentalism. Another is to control consciousness through science. I also have a problem with the assumptions of evolutionary psychology. This is a frightening agenda. Yet another prong is to pretend that philosophy and science is interested in these phenomena in order to promote an atheist takeover of spirituality and a new morality that takes the supernatural out. This has become so pervasive and subtle that people have begun to forget that they are spiritual beings. There is a new threat of the reduction of humans to a race of spiritless zombies serving their elite, technocratic masters who desire to use transhumanism to become overlords and gods.

Therefore, this book is an attempt to engage in an indication of a fairly widespread and perennial pattern, path or way of spiritual evolution. It is sometimes oblique, impressionistic, indicative and suggestive, prompting to engage in consideration of the spirit and consciousness. Certain scientists and academics want to take them away from you. Technological management of human consciousness is the biggest prize. Listen to what some of them actually say. They want to take spirituality and religion out. They want to take the higher dimensions out of morality and replace it with a new scientific 'objective' reality. Then they want to take the Homo out of Homo Sapiens. Humans are merely a dangerous, destructive animal that may be enhanced with technology and altered genetically to cater for 'objectives.' Their genes may be mixed with animals because that is all they are. This is a call to look again. Otherwise ethics will be what they say it is and science has a poor record on that, which it ignores, while gladly attacking religion. We have co-operated enough with our own enslavement.

If you think you heard it all, just ask yourself some questions.

- Do you have a spirit?
- Where did your spirit come from?
- Do you have consciousness?
- Did your consciousness emerge from your brain?
- Is our world an illusory part of a multiverse?
- If you perceive extrasensory things is that not necessarily sensory?
- Can humans govern the world with reason alone?
- Are you comfortable with rule by AI?

The Idea of Accord

'Accord' means agreement and comes from the Latin base of 'to the heart.' It is used as a noun, verb and adjective. An accord could be a legal agreement. It can refer to harmony or being harmonious or being consistent with. One thing may be in accordance with another. A report may be according to some person. Accord is generally used as a positive word. Shakespeare used associated words regularly. In Henry V the French King states in Act V, Scene 11.

> "Plant neighbourhood and Christian-like accord
> In their sweet bosoms, that never war advance,
> His bleeding sword 'twixt England and fair France."

Another word that is close to it is 'correspondence.' Correspondence is a fundamental concept in many esoteric, magical and mystical practices. We have related words like 'according' and expressions like 'of one's own accord. I use it to suggest the need for individual internal accord between who one is and who one wants to be. It suggests the alignment between the head and the heart and the body and the establishment of a 'nexus to the numinous.' It suggests the link between the self, true self, spirit and mind. So accord refers to the purposes of internal journey. Studies such as *The Structure of Magic* by Bandler and Grinder focus on language in therapy. The lesson from such work is how people set up a map of the world based on experience which does not always accord with external reality and how language helps re-align the relationship.

As well as the interior accord there is also an external dimension. The individual must be informed and in accord with the wisdom of the spirit that can always be learned from outside. The individual also seeks to be in accord with the world, cosmos, universal or moral law, highest consciousness, One, the gods or God. There is the accord that can be seen between spiritual traditions. The external accord exists in domains such as the Perennial Philosophy. There is accord between different philosophies. Thus the model here is of an agreement, alignment or accord between will, thought, feeling and philosophy. But to simplify the structure it is as follows.

This book argues that there is a spirit in all of us. Spiritual consciousness is critical. Consciousness is fundamental, pre-existing, permanent and not emergent. Look to science if you think they have a better explanation and you may be surprised to find that they have very little indeed. In our human bodies we develop our self. We can create a false self that is inconsistent with our spirit, that takes us in a direction incompatible with spiritual unfolding and development. The false self may seek false, material satisfaction. We can instead choose to engage in a process of evolution whereby we develop our true self. That is largely a jettisoning of superfluous stuff. It is the rocket ship discarding the rocket necessary to escape the atmosphere. The process of discovering our true self involves an exploration. Compassion is the core value, opposed to hatred and other negative values. This is a discipline of contemplation, experience and reflection. On that journey we focus our attention. Distractions will keep us in the labyrinth. Through this journey we reach further levels. We must learn how to see. We learn what knowledge is and what knowledge is valuable. This is the path of spiritual evolution to the numinous. A nexus is formed at the higher levels. Before spiritual or religious discipline or theology can be implanted there must be the tilled field. The vineyard must be prepared or no seeds can be planted, no growth, no fruits come. Now we have a quantum field. I would argue that the absence of a mystical sense creates angst and ennui that creates an existential despair. Even if it is purely an interior journey and never spoken of to anyone else, it could be the most important pilgrimage one makes. Everyone should continually develop their intellect in parallel. Mysticism is not a substitute but is complementary.

If we avoid the path of growth generally then we are on a slope of spiritual decline. Our lives will be a lottery enslaved in the future to a cruel system with kaleidoscopic changes of objectives. There is a battle posed by materialism, mechanism, scientism, technocracy and intoxication. We can prepare for a new, stripping of the altars. There are right and wrong paths despite the post-modern mind play. I think people have been misled. The word 'accord' also is close to the idea of the 'core' or 'The Core' which sometimes refers to the central experience in Near Death Experiences. The common core theory is also associated with Perennial Philosophy. Thus 'accord' suggests the core associated with mysticism.

Choice of Form and Method: Lines, Sutras, Haikus, Koans, Aphorism, Proverbs, Quotes

This work seemed to come as a mystic gift in parts, though many might not think it so. At the start most lines seemed to emerge into my head and I wrote them down and it grew up thereafter through more considered ways. Some parts are more fixed and many are oblique. Rhythm and metre is often linked to sacred senses. That it is poetic and complex in language indicates the pressure chamber of change we must enter between two worlds. One is fixed, built, logical, useful, methodical and the other is incomprehensible, revealing, informing and inspiring. The origin of words also shows deeper meanings. The title of this book partly suggests what it envisages. There are two elements here, namely the form and the content. As explained above, it engages with mysticism and seeks or suggests the desirability of an accord for the individual. Some lines state propositions as clearly as I can, re-iterating some of the points made here. Some lines are clearly chains in an argument. In relation to form, these lines are described as 'sutras.' Here sutra is used in the sense of the Sanskrit origin of thread, as the basis for an aphorism that can link to a context. They are not haikus in any classic sense but they do have 17 syllables in each line. Traditionalists have a very, specific idea of what a haiku should be, although that has become more elastic in recent times. A 5-7-5 structure obeying certain dictates persists and sticking to that discipline is the beauty of them. Some modern haiku writers have broken all form. Poetic form presents perspectives in unique ways. Poetic philosophy helps with metaphysical matters. The sutras weave a tapestry of meaning. Rumi, the great Sufi mystic, wrote his spiritual couplets. Short statements seem suitable to spiritual scriptures and other such writing. Proverbs and aphorisms are said to use the wit of one person to encapsulate the wisdom of many others. Quotes are similarly useful. So the lines form threads, different in colour and content and what they comprehend. It is interesting that many Irish blessings, often translated, end up a similar length. Old Irish poetry also had a complex sound system perhaps to show that it was not merely normal communication.

Apart from the central theme, I hope many lines can stand on their own, severable and can be re-visited. It is complex and why would it not be? Simplification and reduction loses the possibility of much insight. Word-play is necessary when we need to see things anew and refer to the ineffable. That perspective is based on the mystical tradition. You will find the lines clear, obscure and frustrating. That is part of the way. My model may be Gerard Manley Hopkins. His body lies in Glasnevin Cemetery in Dublin, midway between my infant brother and sister on one side of the graveyard and my parents on the other. I use his poem in the end of this introduction to move between the dimension here and the body of the work. This is my favourite poem in English. I believe it is a poem about the material (leaden) world and the spiritual (golden) world. His technique is not mere ornament. There is something in the 'sprung rhythm' he uses that operates on the subconscious if you allow. Words cast spells.

However sometimes, like a cryptic crossword, there is more meaning hidden. Sometimes there is embedded sense. Sometimes the jarring of words used unusually can allow an idea get past the sentries at the gate of reason. This is the logic of the Buddhist koan. The nature of the koan indicates that the process of reasoning and cognition is limited. The koan often shows how reason finds it hard to breathe in higher dimensions. Taoism and Greco-Roman thought uses epigrams. There is something in the brevity that can penetrate the consciousness like an arrow at times. The Zen approach embraces paradox and uncertainty. Oblique approaches are not necessarily self-indulgent. The limitations of words and thought, to be the being beyond which we inherently know we are, is why such writing appears strange. Sometimes it is better to let the sounds or structure of the words work. We do not seek to analyse too much how a symphony works on us, instead we listen and make assumptions about the motivation of the composer. We do not need to get the meaning to be moved or inspired by the music. We can understand some themes or context. In the West most classic music was spiritually inspired and of spiritual origins anyway. Similarly the experience of the Sunflower paintings defied exact explanation.

Raymond Moody (who developed the term Near Death Experiences) has also emphasised the paradoxical significance of nonsense. He argues that nonsense and unintelligibility are important. Nonsense is not unknowable and not false. Poetry is on the border of unintelligibility too at times. It permeates children's rhymes. It can be seen as deliberate nonsense in Dr. Seuss as distinguished from involuntary nonsense. *Alice in Wonderland* utilises it. Nonsense statement are associated with dying people and the suggestion is that it is about moving between dimensions because the structure of form may be maintained in nonsense. The border of the unintelligibility of the shadowlands is the possibility of indicating states uncommon. Nonsense is beyond sense. One feature of mystical states is their paradoxicality. Poetry in a way allows an oblique approach to truth that works at times better than a head-on approach in the crosswinds. In his book *Finnegans Wake*, James Joyce utilised a complex re-invention of language to create or reflect an altered state of consciousness inventing new words such as 'quark,' which science would later utilise.

I have long argued for a cosmopolitan method that is pragmatic. The view here presented is cosmopolitan in scope. The object is to indicate that the quest for the spirit, and the landmarks on that road, are evident in many traditions. That does not mean that we have to become the other. We learn from other places but must adapt to where we are and enrich it. The quest may lurk in places we have not imagined or that we have forgotten in words, notes or numbers. We have forgotten that alphabet, words and numbers often had mystical significance and origins. The Mystical Accord may seem consistent at times and in some respects with certain streams such as Hermeticism, Prisca Theologia, Rosicrucianism and Transcendentalist philosophy. Aldous Huxley synthesised some streams of thought from around the world and this work has similar sentiments, although his motivations are suspect for me now. Wayne Teasdale and others looked more specifically at mysticism. There are clear echoes of thought from Vedanta and Kashmir Shaivism to Marsilio Ficino to the great Spanish mystical poets. Earlier theosophy shows the pattern. The concepts chime with certain thinkers from Joseph Campbell to Maslow. Ancient Irish thinking is as welcome as Jewish mysticism, if it renders light. Greek and Egyptian myth and philosophy is recurrent. You might see correspondences with the science fiction writer Philip K. Dick, as much as the great student of mysticism Evelyn Underhill or elements of Gnosticism, Buddhist sutras and the Yoga Sutras of Patanjali. All this, because from east, west, north and south there is a remarkable consistency suggesting a path of maturity or evolution of inner life. Details differ significantly but not some basic premises. Nevertheless, it was an approach that emerged from my own inspiration. In essence, the argument here is that there is a common pattern and form of the mystical way. That tradition crosses boundaries and is available to all who are interested in working to attain it. I suggest that the need to reclaim our own spiritual nature is critical at this time of technological advance. It is not New Age because I am not sure what that means, although some might seek to describe it so. It is optimistic about the individual but balanced with a pessimistic warning against scientism, technology and technocracy. I suggest that the mystical tradition reflects a universal trajectory of spiritual evolution that exists across and often in spite of religions. It is there in different traditions because it is in us. The mystical path unites them. The Mystical Accord is a sketch of a map on a transparency that accords with many spiritscapes underneath.

As such, it also fits into the self-development or self-help mode. There are many people who have the capacity to apprehend the significance of such observations without engaging in initiation, submitting to a guru or joining a group. Individuals must engage and own their own development. There are many modes of therapy that pay attention to spiritual life and no one has a monopoly on affairs of the spirit. The approach outlined here involves a commitment to the mystical path (the mystical vocation as Mirandola called it). Here it is called The Mystical Accord. I believe that it represents a re-setting of a range of insights whose recurrence is their validation. In matters of the spirit, there is nothing new under the sun. The threats are unique and perhaps not the ones that people think. The glossary may seem pedantic to some but it offers some help to reduce the uncertainty, especially when many of the terms may seem vague or have multiple or contested meanings. Apologies for any liberties with your cherished concepts. Skip the incomprehensible ones. Good luck.

I finish off here admitting that experience made me look again at Christianity, and that left out of it. I would warn against a purely ego-based self-construction of delusion. Nevertheless, every individual is endowed with spirit that should be allowed to flourish. We should explore and appreciate the nature and phenomenon of spirit and consciousness and protect it vigilantly. We must be careful not to replace sophisticated doctrines with lazy, fuzzy feeling. At the same time, we must be careful to allow people to first find their inner life so it can be cultivated. The aim here is to reflect the pattern of spiritual evolution to emphasise its importance. That aim is not to contradict any religious dogma, save the one that we are gods or God or can become so with the worship of materialism and technology. Strangely, some of the ones who advocate that we are God or gods are the very ones who will deny your spiritual path and take away your consciousness. If someone has strong belief and is attached to a particular dogma then they will not feel threatened. Rather they should consider how the lost are to be found and the impoverished misled by clearly false materialist propaganda. Respect for belief systems is a starting point.

We cede authority ceaselessly to materialism and machines and sacrifice our innate nature, potential and powers for technological adjustments, our soul for a gimmick and our freedom for a bauble, all founded on fantastic fabrications. Most have become cowards to the media's pro-tech, pro-scientism bully pulpit. It may be that the rebels, or the last resistance to technocratic-takeover, speak in poetic language and parables and share humour as freely as they used to, because those things are such as our computer masters and the coded god of reason will find the most difficult to conquer. Why does Dawkins think that a parent communicating their worldview to a child is far more dangerous than the nuclear world run by AI that the scientists are giving us? If people believe in a more complex world, it does not mean they reject science or certain theories. The Mystical Accord is not about whether you believe in God or whether it is necessary to do so. Neither does it suggest that we embark on a quest to contact spirits. It does however more modestly suggest that there is a universal stream of evidence suggesting the mystical spiral to the castle keep of one's own spiritual consciousness. I am also wary of mysticism being employed as a foundation for 'social justice' where the end is a narrow political one which is essentially materialist. That does not mean that it stays remote, only that other motivations should not hijack individual spiritual development.

The recognition of the existence of the treasure chamber space is the object of the guerrilla warfare of the spirit. If we are not to allow 'whatever is fast-flying of us' to be mechanised, we must wake up. Poets know the mystic world. You see it in Antonio Machado's poem *Anoche Quando Dormía*, translated for example to *Last Night as I Slept* or *Last Night as I Lay Sleeping*. The night before as he lay sleeping, he dreamt that a fountain or a spring was flowing in his heart. He wonders from what hidden source this water (from which he had never drunk before) had come. It was a beautiful blessed illusion or vision. Then he dreamt he had a hive of honey bees making golden honey from his past failures. Then he dreamt that a sun was shining in his heart like a hearth giving warmth and light and bringing tears to his eyes. These marvellous illusions or visions make him feel a divine source. This poem has the heart of the mystical experience in it. Keats wrote about 'Fancy' (imagination) in The Realm of Fancy:

> "Open wide the mind's cage-door.
> She'll dart forth, and cloudward soar.
> O sweet Fancy! Let her loose,
> Summer's joys are spoilt by use..."

Wordsworth wrote in The Inner Vision:

"Whate'er the senses take or may refuse,-
The Mind's internal heaven shall shed her dews
Of inspiration on the humblest lay."

These poets knew how potent the imagination was. Others saw the imagination as leading upwards to the divine. The best expression of this is Hopkins. The first part of Hopkins' poem below is his despair with the material world and the inevitable decay of the body:

The Leaden Echo and the Golden Echo

How to keep- is their any any, is there none such, nowhere know
some, bow or
Brooch or braid or brace, lace, latch or catch or key to keep
Back beauty, keep it, beauty, beauty, beauty....from vanishing away?
O is there no frowning of these wrinkles, ranked wrinkles deep,
Down? No waving off of these most mournful messengers, still
messengers, sad and
Stealing messengers of grey?
No there's none, there's none, O no there's none,
Nor can you long be, what you now are, called fair.
Do what you may do, what, do what you may,
And wisdom is early to despair:
Be beginning; since, no, nothing can be done
To keep at bay
Age and age's evils, hoar hair,
Ruck and wrinkle, drooping dying, death's worst, winding sheets,
tombs and worms
and tumbling to decay;
So be beginning, be beginning to despair
O there's none, no, no, no there's none;
Be beginning to despair, to despair
Despair, despair, despair, despair

Then from the despair is a magical, mystical transition or remembrance which is the spirit, the Golden Echo. As a Catholic he places God above, but it works for other ways of seeing.

The Golden Echo

Spare! There is one yes I have one (Hush There!)
Only not within seeing of the sun,
Not within the singeing of the strong sun
Tall sun's tingeing or treacherous the tainting of the earth's air
Somewhere elsewhere there is ah well where! one,
One. Yes I can tell such a key I do know such a place,
Where whatever's prized and passes of us, everythings that's fresh and
fast-flying of us,
Seems to us sweet of us and swiftly away with, done away with, undone
Undone, done with, soon done with and yet dearly and dangerously sweet
Of us, the wimpled-water-dimpled, not by morning-matched face
The flower of beauty, fleece of beauty too too apt to ah! to fleet.
Never fleets more, fastened with the tenderest truth
To its own best being and its loveliest of youth: it is an everlastingness
of O! it is an all youth!
Come then, your ways and airs and looks, locks, maiden gear, gallantry
and gaiety and grace,
Winning ways, airs innocent, maiden manners, sweet looks, loose
locks, long locks,
lovelocks, gaygear, going gallant, girlgrace-
Resign them, sign them, seal them, send them, motion them with breath,
And with sighs soaring, soaring sighs deliver
Them; Beauty-in-the-ghost, deliver it, early now, long before death
Give beauty back, beauty, beauty, beauty, back to God, beauty's self
and beauty's giver
See; not a hair is, not an eyelash, not the least lash lost; every hair
Is, hair of the head, numbered.
Nay, what we had lighthanded left in surly the mere mould
Will have waked and have waxed and have walked with the wind what
while we slept,
This side, that side hurling a heavyheaded hundredfold,
What while we, while we slumbered
O then, weary then why should we tread? Oh why are we so
Haggard at the heart, so care coiled, so care-killed; so fagged,
so fashed, so cogged, so cumbered.
When the thing we freely forfeit is kept with fonder a care,
Fonder a care kept than we could have kept it, kept
Far with fonder a care (and we, we should have lost it) finer, fonder
A care kept- Where kept? Do but tell us where kept, where-
Yonder- What high as that! We follow now we follow-Yonder, yes
yonder, yonder,
Yonder.

Chapter 1

Spiritual Evolution

1.1   On Evolution of Spirit and Mysticism

There are many ways to the Way and many ways away are there.

We must participate, live and function in the real world as it is.

We must appreciate without doubt the tools and things we find out.

We must surely treasure nature about that nurtures us with pleasure.

We must seek our daily bread and build good relations around us.

We must adapt, survive and prosper dealing with existential threats.

We must inform, develop and discipline our mind consistently.

We should appreciate great advances available at this time.

We can however sleepwalk to oblivion, incarceration.

We are all beings who are being literally dispirited.

We are becoming marionettes performing for unknown masters.

Others tax and may play Icarus whose wax will melt above us.

Daedalus constructed a technological labyrinth for us.

Psyche has been pacified to promote a subservient people.

The Age of Enlightenment was not about enlightenment at all.

A mistaken sense of theory of evolution is destructive.

Existence without any enlightenment is a very heavy price.

Evol-ution is calculated to literally invert love.

'Immaterial' means non-material also irrelevant.

Manifestation of stalled spiritual evolution exists.

Millions of war ghosts press against the pane of presence to admonish.

Deliberate, selfish involution of the spirit unfolds.

There has been a certain failure of spiritual evolution.

The meaning of spiritual consciousness is missed and misplaced.

Spiritual concepts constantly inverted looted with jackboots.

If spirit is banished from human evolution it is not us.

Spirit is no mere embellishment, no garish garnish on life's dish.

Many have been hypnotised and mesmerised into oblivion.

Some are drugged, soporific, diverted, drifting without an anchor.

There has been a long winter of the human heart in times of plenty.

The land is dark and such light as is is false and artificial.

We make a fetish of technology and relinquish deep needs.

While we live in senses, the sensory world is blemished, degraded.

Technology and science furnish the fabric of reality.

Science and philosophy now rely on famishing of spirit.

Scientism wants to mock and make our spirit unbeknownst to us.

Current thinking seeks to send spirit on its rip current to the end.

The sacred is set aside by the secular and scientism.

The Unbeknownst cannot be known when spirit is unbeknownst.

Propagandistic philosophy projects profane pro-pagan da.

Institutions that deal with the spiritual have been tarnished.

Spiritual institutions vanish are hijacked and subverted.

Spirit just a superstition, millions for millennia misled?

Stop, stop and listen! Spirit exists and evolves as the world revolves.

Spirit real, burnished, experiences exalted things.

We are inhabited by spirit bathed in I at behind I.

We are spiritual beings here, creatures with spirit within us.

Even if you don't believe in spirit remember that others do.

Dismiss spirit, esoterica, you must discard, miss much great art.

Mind may realise that the eternal existence of being is.

Stein wrote that grace is experienced as an innermost indwelling.

Rule of journey's school is to nourish your own spirit then unfooled.

Spiritual growth shouldn't involve tricks or be accelerated.

Charlatans, frauds, false mediums do not invalidate spirit.

If Houdini exposed falsehood that is good but it does not end it.

Spirit efflorescence, unbrutish, is of the essence in this life.

Perils come from the root 'to try,' anguish abates when the pearl is sought.

Create from the clandestine record then an accord with destiny.

Engage the ethereal from the ephemeral and etherised.

Every individual has the need to re-furbish their spirit.

Without a way of the spirit we are bewildered and misplace it.

Being bewildered we will be wont to be beguiled and bewitched.

Beholding we behold so that our gifts belonging are not begone.

Beyond is where we came from and worldly were wordily beckoned back.

Blandishments of the outlandish are bland dish compared with beyond.

The mystical path is a universal one that has been hidden.

Mysticism deals with the mysterious and the revelation.

Mystics seek personal, direct communion with highest consciousness.

The mystical trajectory is inscribed in us to manifest.

We miss the mystical paths in mists of the obscure and occult.

Sutras, aphorisms, clues, koans, paradox and haiku form direct.

The sutra is art to us to use to utter the sacred and sane.

Mansions of meaning may be made brick by brick, many aphorisms.

If you think there's nothing higher than you, still cherish highest that's true.

To induce indwelling well we wander yonder with own wonder won.

Suggestion and confusion can sometimes better slip by the mindguard.

Wisdom from wherever found, the strangest people, places world around.

Balance, harmony of the whole person come from the call of spirit.

Art of spirit is the spirit of art and part of the whole with rest.

All spiritual traditions have a core of higher encounter.

Primordial, perennial, pre-ordained, ur, prototypical.

A waste land is destiny of solely, externally embedded.

Exclusive explanation of highest spirit punishes learning.

Win though utter truth through a glass darkly, insight-starkly true window.

Mystic pattern is ever recurrent, consistent, imperishable.

Mystic ways may not all travel but life's riddles we can unravel.

Beyond any mess, great traditions of spirit stress the same message.

Gnomes we think homed within and without may be trapped in gnomes of ink.

That spirit should spirally evolve requires it be admitted.

Evolution of spirit only occurs in individuals.

Evolution of individual spirit is to unity.

You are spirit that will persist even if you are an atheist.

Even if you think the grave the end the spirit should to joy extend.

Seek sources of solace solely within rather than being soulless.

Joy deep and replenishing is the promise then of mystic's keep.

Spirit spirals with mystic winds upwards and back to spirit's source.

Spirit destiny is not a jack o' lantern in a stagnant swamp.

Spirit must soar and not harsh remain a marsh light on the forest floor.

Being bewildered out of moorings we are led through storms to sail on.

Will is then the stirrup to mount the purist pursuit of the spirit.

1.2   The Spirit. What is it?

These sutras seek to evoke and invoke a mystical accord.

Mysticism is in the province of the spirit convinced of it.

Mysticism that denies spirit is a sailor denying a ship.

Mystic sticks, adheres to the spirit, stick up for it here as time ticks.

Spirit is the invisible force which permeates the universe.

Spirit it is the unity within us that always persists beyond.

Spirit is pure, ur, primal, there always, obscured it is cured with care.

Spirit is ideal form of you immaterial, abstractable.

Spirit wisdom has evolved just like scientific knowledge has done.

Spiritual consciousness comes from experience and evidence.

Spirit here is bigger than soul and independent of the body.

Spirit may be the light body that can rise like the eagle upwards.

Spirit is enhanced consciousness, whatever is fast-flying of us.

Born we are borne to this dimension with a draught of forgetfulness.

Some call the soul that which detaches and experiences this life.

Still inside there resides a tide that tidies and will take you elsewhere.

Once upon a time, spirit was not a stranger nor a fantasy.

Like from inside a spider was spun the silk that captured life's meaning.

Spirit had not been sent spiralling in the smoke of mass machines.

Spirit had not yet been dismissed, discounted, denied, denigrated.

Spirit had not yet been monopolised, marshalled, marched, made to die.

Mystics all emphasise paramount significance of the spirit.

Mystics often thought the way was unsuitable to many people.

Mystics mostly accept that all have a spiritual calling kept.

Without finity there is no infinity, finity in it.

Spiritual evolution uses inner for exterior.

Spirit, pure awareness is nature of the creature we are, become.

Psychic health requires a whole conception of the growth of spirit.

If you have no spirit what are you but a slave of circumstance?

Spirit is enfolded, compressed, concentrated and may be opened.

Spirit is inner airbag, life ring, life jacket for the muddled mind.

Flesh is the mesh of spirit, fresh home for the recurrent, old being.

An essence, a seed, bud, formula, message lie within us all.

Fear, doubt, anxiety and procrastination keep spirit dormant.

Some say that other spirits can inhabit inhibit and haunt us.

Mind can make spirit hibernate and ignore the rays of springtime.

Every individual has a deep, un-explored potential.

Resisting summonings of spirit we seek comfort in thoughts and things.

There is a force to the spirit for recognition or repulsion.

The nature of spirit includes the spirit of nature and its life.

Ego in control is formula for spiritual perdition.

Perdition is loss of potential of expansion, liberation.

Ego often sacrifices heart and soul to win something instead.

In spiritual evolution, the lonely step is important.

As well as 'as above so below' so as within, so without.

A quiet life of nature and nurture may be a bright path for some.

A wild life of exploration of boundaries may work for others.

A person of action that realises may realise well.

Passivity from the Latin 'to suffer.' It causes suffering.

We can be pacific without being passive or violent.

Intellect and reason are valuable zones as part of a whole.

Intellect without intuition languishes about in trouble.

Inscape, insight, inspiration, invention, instinct, intellect.

Cosmic consciousness comes into cosmopolitan understanding.

Cosmos is macrocosm-manifested man as microcosm.

The time for spiritual divisiveness has long then departed.

The big threat to your spirit are people who seek to deny you it.

Some seek to ridicule and deride the very idea of spirit.

The mystic need not be inoffensive or passive before power.

We can be tough mentally while peaceful but resisting outside.

Different paths, apparently diverse may converge with compass.

The fountainhead, through Aries, the cycle of meaning begins for some.

Of the awakenings, the first that must occur is that of spirit.

Spirit sounds that recur in language are the remnants of the ur.

Demons demonstrate strata at odds that would stop your spirit growing.

Definition is a limited tool where discounting makes the fool.

What religion seeks to oppose the thaw of spirit having frozen?

If you can, conceive Atman to Brahman, One, God, the Great Spirit.

For some, quantum coherence may provide a conception to work with.

Spirit is the breath, beat, best of you not to be denied till you die.

Get a sense of its kind so as not to let your tense mind forget it.

Sound causes or leaves shape whether you believe we came from ape or not.

Source is the ore within us all, a real resource in our core to care.

Do not wait for near death experiences to realise spirit.

You do not need draughts or strange brews to seek after spirit in you.

Let goodwill infuse all your being and your doing and your spirit.

There is always a level drawing above where we are, move, perceive.

Sequence, sequel, segue so seem sequestered in sage spirals.

It is elementary, we're meant to discover what is in us.

It is not other spirits but your own to be known, own and find all.

".. so no one deceives you and says 'Look over here!' or 'Look over there!'"

It is there to seek, nowhere else, your innermost ghost, guessed guest.

Spirit, something, everything or nothing consciously, unconsciously.

Be not scared or scarred but dare care your dear sacred to secede.

Engage mind with these sutras to enter the strata beyond thought.

Pieces of the puzzle are sewn on patchwork quilt of people's story.

Pick everything apart that departs from your view and makes your wasteland.

Joy, calm, peace and lightness is our essence. Spirit is power and force.

Blake wrote that everything that lives is holy. We are that. Spiritus.

Without spirit we feel and fail to make sense of great bewildering.

Spirit is the castle keep that keeps at bay the sweep of sensation.

1.3   Consciousness. What is it? Where does it come from?

Spirit is the human insufflation of the cosmic consciousness.

Spirit is your own awareness, being, consciousness, full and complete.

Satchitananda is the being consciousness bliss in us of us.

You are aware. Awareness unwearable. Divest what you were.

Sentience, senses sent not by time and space necessarily bent.

All that we have been and are is within us to access to avail.

Diverse ideas are consistent with a simple sense of being.

Do you believe that consciousness is a mere accident, trick, falsehood?

The ones who said they were enlightened then took away enlightenment.

Consciousness was reduced by enlightened, illumined science thinkers.

Consciousness became craggy rock pools of crabs cut off from ocean tide.

Consciousness as a concept is a chameleon moving quickly.

Consciousness is capacity for experience of aware self.

Be not blinded, bamboozled, lured to believe it is not there behind.

Consciousness oozes through you and those who share this beautiful affair.

Consciousness is field with intelligence and inter-relationships.

Consciousness is not pertaining to you but you pertaining to it.

The inner life involves recognition of the gift of consciousness.

Pure consciousness is what is in us, we are part of, but we obscure.

Born with mystic instinct we are taught thereafter to demystify.

Imagining and intention are the acts that can become facts.

Imagining is magic reflecting great, mighty imagining.

For some there's a skylight to beyond in the highest of the human.

Many explorers believe that everyone can rise above time, space.

Many rose to places even with celestial landscape then seen.

Between consciousness in universe, beyond, abroad, be awed with bond.

Consciousness can transcend boundaries the mind and body conceives.

Consciousness is capable of great expansion and much enhancement.

Consciousness in us rises to the non-local, light as an angel.

Our consciousness incarnates replicating bigger pattern in us.

Consciousness incarnate is ocean wave's breaker white horse meet mate meat.

Consciousness and spirit should correspond or your existence is all.

Consciousness entails possibility of growth and development.

Consciousness involves perception, potential and possibility.

Consciousness though settled in us reigns but recalls its greater domain.

Consciousness has continuity and in us is contained careful.

Aspiring to higher consciousness is needed to evolve.

Non-ordinary, extraordinary states were ordinary.

Higher and lower consciousness exist, it is better to ascend.

High here has what we are and have been but falling into flesh forget.

On the way of all flesh we intrude knowing fantastic interlude.

Consciousness aspiring must be inspiring and not heartless.

Why stay agitated outside the gates of ascending consciousness?

Perennial, mystical traditions provide a sound, framework.

Consciousness of other people's gods cannot threaten that you believe.

Your Almighty does not need protection from you or it is not It.

You must though have force to fight or resist for else you lose resources.

Sutra is the Sanskrit for 'thread.' Suture ruptures in spirit therewith.

The original is not that with the sin in but it is our source.

When we begin to relinquish our beginning it begs the question.

Beautiful being beginning, buried or belittled brings bandits.

Be aware of your awareness beyond reach of each, everyone else.

Aware of consciousness, awareness or remain in maya, matrix.

Consciousness is sensational but is it mere sensation to you?

Some scientists think consciousness is mere excrescence, like a wart.

Some say spirit is sump, we are all then sumph, just fit to be sumpter.

Consciousness and spirit caused science. Oedipus seeks to kill the king.

Consciousness matters more to the brain than grey matter will do to it.

They look for consciousness but it may be water hidden in water.

It may be in the quantum domain they think they will find the answers.

Microtubules, hyperspace, synapses, collapsing wave functions.

Science may never quite get it and what they do get will not be it.

That which is a great problem for science is but our great potential.

Consciousness, spirit are in us, there, the sum of all parts.

Consciousness is primary, spirit is prime, find your primordial.

Consciousness in its nature is perpetual and perennial.

It is in you always from before until then after you are it.

It will not be taken away as it is no matter what they may say.

It is the general genius of you that sits in the gene's nest.

It is not a flesh genie lain nor a selfish gene getting laid.

Seed gives sunflowers turning to the sun only with the in-between.

What is there in us must tend to the Whatever above to the end.

Flower has the seed but is not it, you have the gene but are not it.

There are types of consciousness in us but the central one came before.

Pearl real in perennial, leper not repelled, reap, replevin soul.

Padma in the pantheon, patriarchy, Phoebus, paeon of you.

Pallas Athena in you, pregnant, the prepared promised land of you.

Perennial sum, I am, recurrent, persistent, persevering.

Prepossessing, preposition, in, on, with, by, across, up, through us.

Prelapsarian, pre-personal pronoun in plethora of you.

Primate, consciousness, prized, emergent, put in us, inspired.

Pristine pert, in stripe, in sprite, inspire, prius then propagating.

Plenipotentiary priority, potentate replenishing.

Plenum, plenar, plenitude producing all that may be possible.

Premise of promise, pressed, presumed, prevailing over pretexts.

Primal spirit is sought, discovered, found to replace conscious spirit.

Preserved in us, pale but still in words and practices from our past.

Precinct of instinct, unpriested palace, precious prophet postulant.

Prototypical, from the pattern that is us, is in us, assured.

Pre-conceptual, projecting before the plaid of our position.

Presence of the permanent in us, the pre-sent, present presence.

Primeval preparation priming us there neither prim nor prissy.

Preliminary consciousness is perfect in its existence.

Pure consciousness is our origin and the end we must re-unite.

Psyche in its purest form inured in you still resting, the best.

Primitive, imitative, potent with portents, prodigy placed.

Precious is the principal power, precedence you preside over.

Principled you are president over the state of your reality.

Principality is you, in you drawn, governed by you, not pawned.

Premier, premium airier without need of consortium.

Pregnant, we are protean, poised with plosive possibilities.

Programmed therein is the part of you that is, has been and so can be.

Protagonist is you, the prequel you write or re-write with power.

Protoplasm of the spirit is the only way across the chasm.

Pride of place in us is the pure spark, seed and the preternatural.

Pure consciousness in us is what is cosmic creating, vital life force.

Profundity of presence in you prepared to produce from there.

Purification is just taking out impostures to enrapture.

The point, spark is the centre of us and completed, is the monad.

Periphery always needs the support of the centre as Dee says.

Primary is experience for us, provisional the culture.

End so we begin, so as not to circle around like a shark fin.

Enough, there is in us from the start that which is all if we open.

End the emergency of emerged emergent explanations.

Archetypal, enduring in our treasury there to be drawn on.

Avatars and angels are awaiting attention of what's in us.

Above arrogant simple, 'self' consciousness is cosmic consciousness.

Mystics through the inner pinhole can sense the whole of pure consciousness.

In the sweatlodge native peoples learned separable, conscious spirit.

On the death bed, out of body, hypnotised, dreaming, the veil lifts.

Ingenious, genius within the genus of intention.

Mysticism is the quest to find a way back, or out, to truth state.

Spirit combining love, consideration is force of universe.

Consciousness causes a compulsion for the circle of completion.

Altered states of consciousness are real, dear altars whereon to taste.

Consciousness may make and erase time and space and we have got it wrong.

Some think non-local consciousness is that which comes into our spirit.

The completion you need is the return to seed point like in monad.

To some there was a prisca theologia that was core of all.

Some say there was an ancient, universal theology since lost.

Some think theology is just a fantasy made up by the brain.

Some think theology and free will delusions that must go away.

Model makers that claim that much is delusion ignore it within.

Mysticism is more empirical than materialism.

However limited, circumscribed we have free will in us inscribed.

Universal laws are written into the cosmos not made by man.

There must be a zenith somewhere, something above which there is nothing.
Sutras are curt structure to cut and cure truth into stepping stones.

1.4 Compassion. The Important Way

Stir your hiding heart to recognise and engage the highest of all.
Self compassion and to others and to ourself when others we wound.
Your mind misleadingly make mistakes that cause suffering mind can cure.
Our acts have foreseeable consequences, responsible are we.
Sense of prevention of suffering of others instilled makes most sense.
Mysticism graces compassion and it graces mysticism.
Compassion cleanses the lenses of spiritual apprehension.
Compassion is then not unconcern, coldness, cruelty, callousness.
The way that does not involve compassion is not to the higher realm.
Because we interpenetrate the world of others we will feel them.
Imagination is the gift of consciousness, path is empathy.
Inner power is phenomenal, philosophy impoverished.
Intuition is a suppressed skill like other of our lost senses.
Ingenuity with insight can triumph over ignorance.
Immutable is the sign of compassion in passing circumstance.
Compassion is the mirror of the extent of your self perception.
In Upanishads 'dayadhvam' Eliot called to heal the waste land.
We are losing basic, day-to-day recognition of other life.
There is a twinkle in the eye whose dwindling belies advance.
Empathy is not about using someone else's pain for gain.
Empathy is not merely acquiescence and accommodation.
Empathy and compassion isn't mere pity but supportive feeling.
Empathy to be a true quality must involve true difference.
Empathy deeply felt and sought may not appear so prettily wrought.
True compassion may not advertise and not come in expected ways.
It is foolish to ignore that there is destructive consciousness.

Like a faun of beast and spirit we choose the dimension we tend towards.

Why consciousness is destructive or how labelled is less important.

Should we feel more care for the psychopath or the potential victim?

That which may be arrogant, controlling, cruel and mean is not the way.

Active connection between the heart and cosmos is a special key.

Compassion to oneself and others is the soil of toil of spirit.

Compassion by rote unfeeling is not the route of growth of spirit.

Compassion is not mere capitulation without any challenge.

Ritual without spirit is a play in a graveyard of symbols.

Space for self allows knowledge without distraction to find feelings soar.

Vision is spiritual evolution through self-integration.

We underestimate our potential, overestimate problems.

From convoluted argument to convolution, evolution.

From the convention, conventicles to contours and connections.

Failure to conquer yourself means you become conquered by others.

Finally there is no inside, no outside just asides at stages.

Discipline allows learning, concentration and balance in growth.

Spiritual evolution must start on the inside of the self.

The art of the ur is in us, in sutra to use to fuse to light.

When the self becomes true or real self, it will blossom like a flower.

With growth in size, appreciation happens that couldn't otherwise.

Compassion encompasses the heart so darkness then will it bypass.

Compassion is the mystic chord in the melody of consciousness.

Revolutions bring back to the same place. Do evolution instead.

Awareness of consciousness can facilitate living consciously.

On earth you must afford yourself an aery accord towards the heavens.

Your chief responsibility is to respect majesty of life.

Ahimsa is a principal articulation of principle.

Compassion is field of mutual recognition of suffering.

The spirit and consciousness are like clouds and rain, water and the wave.

The neighbour, do unto others as you wish to be done to yourself.

The chief opportunity is to explore the range of your powers.

The mystical path is one open to the ready heart and mind.

If a person is destructive to self, others, facilitate not.

All foundation must be based on healing, non-harm without confusion.

If your mystic spirit loves death it is not the path herein met.

The mystic will not fear death nor grasp too long when the time is come.

Keep your feet deep on the earth and don't yield to dearth of discipline.

We realise we are more than we have thought, than we have been told.

Crook of compassion symbol is to help others and your lower self.

You are called a fool if you allow that such thing as spirit can rule.

Does spirit exist, does consciousness exist? Why? What are they?

The iconic rubicon is belief in spirit and consciousness.

Sceptical of spirit on what base lies the concept of dignity?

Spirit, self-gathering clarification and growth go together.

Spirit belief does not have to be elaborate, structured, but be.

Spiral spiritual movement can occur, entrance point varies.

Spiritual consciousness being whole, core of concentric circles.

Since time immemorial remaining in us is the spirit being.

Like with wick in wax or tallow, the spirit is the flame that hallows.

Learn to breathe and you can earn to read and apply the book of spirit.

Your every breath of fresh air yet comes there and with joy should be met.

Religions were founded on mysticism and then sacrificed it.

'I forgive all living beings may all living beings forgive me.'

But then punishment in not inconsistent with human dignity.

And eyes then realise the hand of mercy is never merchandise.

"It droppeth as the gentle rain from heaven upon the place beneath."

We are shadows, vanishing vapours on windowpane a snowy night.

We find the deep magic universe in us with keys of compassion.

Irony of what we trust of us is dust and like iron must rust.

We all are given short shrift, so you use the time to find your gift.

With lush grass of hushed morning sun we are dew all diamonds that vanish.

1.5 Mysticism

What is the meaning of the word mysticism? It is what it is.

You do not have to look like or be a Mahatma to be mystic.

Facility for mystical experience is a human gift.

Mysticism recognises spiritual possibility.

Mystics or experiencers do not have to outwardly show it.

Mystics may be silent for words do not work to describe what it was.

Mystics may be silent because they are made to be mad by many.

Mystical experiences may then happen to anybody.

Mystical attention, discipline, commitment may deepen after.

Mysticism allows mystics to use capacity for insight.

Mystics have mystical experiences and mystical states.

Mystical states are usually then altered states of consciousness.

Mystical states have a range by whose degree the person will change.

Mystical states specific create a general state pacific.

Mystical states loses self, escapes time and space, allow a merging.

Mystical states leave the self behind and sense boundaries expanding.

Mystical states feel beyond you, unifying and interacting.

Mystical states may occur without religion or even spirit.

A mystical experience usually leaves a transforming mark.

Mark of mystical transformation does not die nor dwindle with time.

In mysticism to trust, to seek to define and describe we must.

It comes between myself, mystery and mystify, mystique, myth.

Mystagogue, an initiator into religious mysteries.

Mysticism often relates to mystery or sacred secret.

Mysticism is the origin of the concept of mystery.

Mystes in Greek the priest who manages the secret ceremonies.

Mysterion, mysteria, secret rites and doctrines, mystery religions.

Myein also meant closed or shut and may have been related for some.

Mysterium in Latin. Mistere French and a mixture in Hebrew.

It may mean something holy which is hidden from ordinary people.

It may, as a state, refer to a euphoric or high, serene one.

It may specifically refer to state of union with the divine.

It may refer to the ante-chamber of presence of the divine.

It may refer to a state of union with nature or consciousness.

It may be opening to nothingness, the Void, dazzling darkness.

It may be seeing inside of your being and others and things.

It may refer to other dimensions, versions of reality.

It may come as present, physiology, psychedelics, practice.

It may occur in a wide range of different, diverse circumstances.

It may come about when parts of the brain's functions are quietened.

It may come when you move attention from the brain's back to the front.

It may be the opening of valves of feeling beyond the normal.

It may involve the sudden, strange influx or download of knowledge.

It is said to come from different roots in the Greek language and others.

It may come from the word for an initiate, or verb to conceal.

It seems to be related to meaning to induct or introduce.

It could easily be said to be same word, meaning as mystery.

It is consistently meant to link to something that seems hidden.

It does not deny reality but seeks to extend, expand it.

It is a powerful force of spirit that takes you out of yourself.

It refers to the highest, peak, spiritual experiences.

It is sacred and blissful, reverent, entrancing and compelling.

It is the joy of being really at home and wanting to stay there.

It may disturb sometimes but peace is destined to come about from it.

It may lead to a lifting of the reality veil forever.

It will change the way you see the world and how you will conduct your life.

William James saw religious experience, oneness including God.

It is clear mystics recur and have similar experiences.

Mystical experiences are the highest that many can have.

Mystics find that a more vivid reality of being exists.

Mystics learn something they do not forget and would not have got elsewhere.

Mystics find meaning that gives tranquility and peace and life energy.

But mystics make mayhem and mistrust in the minds of many of us.

Critics of mysticism have much to say, their own fears to allay.

Mysticism may seem like mischief or madness to many people.

They may say that mysticism cannot be proven objectively.

They may say that it is opposed to reason and rationality.

They may say it is nonsensory and therefore that it is nonsense.

They may say it is unreliable fantasy or counterfeit.

They may say that such experiences are just interpretations.

They may say it does not exist as they can not experience it.

They may say that it is too vague to have any meaning that works.

They may say that it is merely word-constituted experience.

They may say that it is merely constructed out of people's upbringing.

They may say that mysticism is a disease of the brain or mind.

They may say it is evolutionary left overs in the brain.

They may say mysticism should be kept only for special elites.

They may say that mysticism is an illusion of no value.

They may say mysticism is dangerous delusion causing death.

They say mystical is imagined with no other reality.

They say that mysticism must be measurable to have meaning.

They say that academics cannot agree on what it is about.

They say that absent science and objectivity it is not real.

They say that only certain types are legitimate and valid ones.

They may say that mysticism is satisfied through religion.

They may say the common core of mysticism robs their uniqueness.

Many think reality they find laid, not that it is of mind made.

Mysticism is indeed the very origin of all religion.

Mysticism then becomes marginalised made merely mythical.

Mysticism is not owned by any other groups outside of you.

Mysticism is the spring, source, sun that illuminates in the heart.

Mystic discipline is secret aqueduct we may build to the heart.

Mysticism is recurrent, persistent, consistent, ancient.

Mysticism creates a mirror of material vanity.

Mysticism is meaningful for us and for all of our people.

Mysticism subjective can cross the bridge to objectivity.

Mysticism even if 'just imagined' has real consequences.

Mysticism is might in us, meant to be milked by us and for us.

Mysticism is path or journey that can be the way for many.

Mysticism speaks of a pattern of practice to attain a peak.

Mysticism is the spirit path beyond materialism.

Mysticism is the power of the prophet to pierce and perceive.

Mysticism need not be overwhelming but made there for our help.

Mysticism is surmounting of the illusion of time and space.

For some who might not get it Star Wars force for light may point to it.

You see it in many great people who do things but don't proclaim it.

Look for it in warriors, leaders, saints, inventors, poets, painters.

Focus, tend reality of process of the mystic, not the end.

Provisioned is us, provided, all the possibilities we need.

'The true light that gives light to everyone was coming into the world.'

As our galaxy became the Milky Way is mysticism made.

Do not let the hawkers at the sacred site confuse or mislead you.

The hawk flies down to you and your mind senses its qualities and gifts.

'Take no part in fruitless evil works but rather instead expose them.'

Mystics false make fools of real vision and turn away those disposed.

Mystics must surmount reason but really resort to it in season.

Mystics must in visions trust but to others then their world turn again.

Mystics are not escapists but venturing beyond in time respond.

Mystics make punctures in the pretensions of pretend reality.

Mystics simplicity shows because from complexity wisdom flows.

When the world wakes a counsel of despair mystics make it out of there.

Chapter 2

Nature of Self

2.1 Self and Superfluous Self

Say we have a general self, having a false self and a true self.

Some say we have no self but we must beware the wares on their shelf.

Some of those who nearly die say there still goes a surviving I.

Some say self is an illusion but who is saying that then to whom?

Self can never be known if we have no self to know of our own.

So look at your self in the round to see thereby what may be found.

Spirit is in soul and self with extra weight from societies shelf.

Superfluous to the true self is the false so we sculpt and pare all.

Self may be the ego to some groups depending on the argot.

Self is like the globe which cannot be seen until we leave it behind.

Seen as spirit or not, self is the lodestar to start from, for, afar.

But we are battered while believing that we are much less than we are.

By being distanced from our being, potential and power we mar.

We shall cast our lot in with fools and fail to marshal ourselves forward.

We may make a future false self that takes us away from our true source.

Tense with trash, dashing, fashed with fashions, awaiting ash of approval.

Bashed, hashed, thrashed, crashed, lashed, mashed, seek the stash of hush.

Brainwashed, heaped with hogwash, leashed, abashed with ennui entrained.

Not crushed but content, satisfied, increase your comprehension.

If lofty wings do not entice, peace of mind is a thing that is nice.

Integrate spirit fragmented or re-visit it to see its soul.

Like Dante we find ourself in a dense wood lost at times, sought or not.

Spiritual emergencies paradoxically allow growth.

Spiritually transformative experiences may create space.

Many crises may be emergency calls of the spirit ignored.

The wounded inner child may lead to the creation of the false self.

Sometimes people need help from experts who know how to help them prosper.

When I am in woodspace pay attention, be calm as it knows my place.

We may feel a force moving us then whence we were to somewhere else.

Self exists in a material world and therein we should prosper.

Survival, challenges of existence, subsistence require growth.

Stagnation of self, forgetting to grow, condemn to unhappiness.

Steady the need to grow, adapt it is ceaseless and incessant.

Self, inflated or fragmented, can great calm find in the mystical.

Retreat from mind to remember being, aware, no object, at times.

Presence, being, awareness of awareness pursued clarifies.

Hence we go hence, with sense and cadence in the dance of the thenceforth.

The mystic is but one path that has ubiquitously not been quit.

Know yourself, to thine self be true, that is the beginning of wisdom.

You create the narrative of you, you write your story of yourself.

You are trained to pleasure that causes pain unless insight you can gain.

Discover who you are meant to be, abandon the pretence you see.

Develop the right hemisphere of your brain and left side and link them.

Events can prompt and point or expectations push to ponder future.

If we cannot the point of spirit see, growing of self must still be.

If the self is un-examined or unknown we cannot then engage.

In Tibetan, basic self is 'sem,' sum of existing external.

Dictionary- word 'baptism' lies between Baphomet and bapu.

The gift of intuition must be acknowledged and developed.

Grow we must by flourishing of love of ourself, others and life.

You watch yourself, observe, recall, analyse, edit, delete and learn.

Your selves are different cells, wherefrom you must be able to escape.

Harmony is living in accordance with the different parts of us.

Lower self allows felt the self taste we loved then hasten to lose.

Look at your self or selves and see the different actors before you.

Like chess be active, control the centre, create space, be vigilant.

Meet the bull in the china shop, the minotaur in the labyrinth.

Around the walls of your thought there are mindwalls of others.

Ouroboros, serpent with tail in its mouth, complete. When does it stop?

Scepticism is useful, intellect must reign in its domain.

See, listen, intuit, discover, step out, do, bear fruit, get over.

Self, the psyche, mind and ego, accumulates negative patterns.

Sit in a room. It is clearly a construct like your thoughts. Go beyond.

See your selves on a stage and as director talk and control them.

The negative, critic that dwells within does not belong on the stage.

Direct the actors in your project within and share your direction.

We are consumers being trained to consume, cannibalise our soul.

We must consciously begin a journey of self-initiation.

We know we must operate within games but still we can come forward.

We have many mansions of selves. Every dog has its day. Know them.

We awaken when we look at self or do so for we awaken.

We avoid the undiscovered continent for silly puppet shows.

We gaze as tourists on platforms over the canyon of our inscape.

We stare at our reflection in the mindwell but don't lower the pail.

We often speak from the brain to entertain and not so we learn.

We concentrate on self so we can rise above it to our primal.

2.2   False Self

The self like a magnet attracts scrap that works it then to entrap.

The parts of self that attaches to things to itself heaviness brings.

Mystical experiences leaves chrysalis of false self behind.

False self is the superfluous to get through then to get to the true.

That we have a false self does not mean that we have no self there at all.

Programmes in you may lead you astray so they must be taken away.

If you live in false self your true self can become a stranger to you.

If in deed or on your way false self becomes leader you go astray.

Memory may make heavy our light body so it cannot rise up.

The death or demise of ego is the way of the mystic to go.

The self is an inner being with an outward crust and atmosphere.

Self is somewhat finite, much of it false, not all fits it or fills it.

Ignorance is facing to an illusory, chimerical self.

False self is avidya produced golem of our real golden goal.

A false self will cause discord, disharmony within and without.

Stories of overcoming the monster are often about ego.

You must know yourself and not create the persona of a stranger.

The self is a mixture, molecule of various compositions.

There is in the self an elf that may need a new home.

Only our body consciousness will be shed like a skin at our death.

One cannot claim to know but no claim to the contrary can be proved.

Out of body experiences are not just anomalies.

Much of that self is threatened by ten thousand traps and tribulations.

Tepid with trepidation we are troubled, torpid, torpedoed.

Make millions, make a killing, but spirit picks skilly in skillion.

Spirit and consciousness, are words to describe self that must journey on.

False self is a matrix that makes a fossil of the spirit in us.

Sentience is not a sentence but with 'I' sense it is, I feel.

Committing to exploring spirit involves an address to the self.

Ask the healing question to escape the waste land and reform the rift.

We may choose or have a journey thrust on us and use darkness to grow.

Soar above the self and sent thus seek to see the essential and rest.

Instead of being fast, having fast-food, fast from food now and then.

If you make your values deeper be sure what you want to invest in.

Immanent means dwelling within. We must dwell there and relate outwards.

Awakening must then occur in relation to reality.

Our outer self may be an hallucination of the true self.

Much is superfluous in what we think is the self that can be lost.

A false persona may coagulate, congeal or be encrusted.

Our imprints create a curtain between the self and its reflection.

Make your set-up much stronger so you cannot be easily upset.

Sage or savage, salve and salvage from the sanctum and sanctuary.

That which is false in us will become a heavy burden for the soul.

Being benevolent evolved is our being not violent.

Laugh, have wit, see comedy, humour, fun, joke, play with your heart intact.

The social self is a balloon that may burst into realisation.

As we are false we relax in a matrix of falsity and vanity.

As lone-lighted ships passing in the night we shout faint in the blackout.

Sunyata, sonatas, become aware of the subtle and skillful.

Set the right tone, then tune in as the medium becomes the message.

Be more skilled with your interactions and how you use your energy.

Make sure that you do not take the wrong path or then practices worsen.

Like a martial artist be calm, composed with uncomfortable onslaught.

Take yourself lightly at times disregarding slights to live in the light.

Medication to meditation is better, changing one letter.

2.3   Attitude of Growing

Instill a sense of calm, tranquility, strength, growth, drop by drop.
No ill in, instill, still in, still till you can distill from the still.
With your will in spirit as your wish then accept not swill as your dish.
Go to soul soil in garden before thoughts, feelings, sensations. Aware.
Growing often feels painful, traumatic, going from darkness to light.
Desire to grow is seed, then the flourishing of that deep wish comes.
You need to be disrupted sometimes. Disruption comes from without.
Be open not gullible, have appetite not apophenia.
Desire is a wild horse you chose to mount whispering, cajoling.
If you can't be on your own, it will be harder to find you have grown.

To grow we link with growing things, open our sensitivity.

Study the power and different techniques of breathing, breath spirit.

Spirit is dynamic, expanding or contracting and retreating.

Seek the sattva, minimise tamas, manage rajas, find direction.

Seek soon air, sun, sea, lake, mountain, forest, desert, garden, stars and moon.

State your state to yourself and create and change your state to suit growth.

Separate thinking and emotion when it is required to be.

Look within for the ruby, the cinnabar wherefrom quicksilver comes.

Thinking changes feelings, emotions. Think well, positively, happy.

Make up your own mind, follow your star, march to the beat of your own drum.

Look at your habits, mental habitats and change them to suit yourself.

We don't deny the darkness within but recognise and amend it.

Try to accept, be at ease, have grace, be very comfortable.

Learn to do well and do well and dwell well on it welling within you.

Kindness is the glue that covers the cracks in fragments of being.

Ancient Greeks thought of human flourishing and virtue as important.

Eudaimonia usually had an inner harmony in.

Inner harmony involves having no more harm in you to project.

No ill will, no poison in the soul, but no ingratiation.

Good humour but not belittling people or being belittled.

You must struggle and be combative in protection of your being.

If you adjust your self you become sceptical of other facades.

Be enthusiastic, especially with challenges encountered.

We treat people openly and humbly, alert to destructiveness.

Jolly up, why not? Come on. You might as well. Don't give up. Keep right on.

The attitude of rising above self is inner transcendence.

With no hither and tither, no here and there of movement, we wither.

Within, we must become director of orchestra of destiny.

Introspection can help create exploration and explanation.

Contemplation is a temple to construct and enter at our will.

Still, relaxed, tranquil, screen blank, new images seen, hidden, unbidden.

Stillness is a non-grasping, non-yearning, non-quaking calmness of now.

Go to the right, placid state, without fear the archetypes will appear.

Be fit in mind, body, spirit, not fitting in is the big sin.

Observe, look, see, study, watch, perceive, persevere, explore and listen.

Eros, vitality, life-affirming set, the unknown direction met.

Fix broken spokes in the wheel for it must be really whole for its role.

To reach equilibrium we must consider the depths on both sides.

Real alms on the altar of self alters material realms.

Nurture, nutrition ur ur nature out, ut, utter truth, turn, et tu.

Unless past problems persist that you need to attend let them end.

Acknowledge the perversity, weakness, fear, darkness over the edge.

Accept that the two came from one, duality, yin yang, Gemini.

Awakenings show the way to the latest wait, next gate, future fate.

2.4   Purify. The Need to Subtract

How we behave, bad habits we save, need not follow to the grave.

Possibility and potential is always there and the past not.

People can never be perfect but can purify their potential.

If not able to bend or too straight we may end up as evil's bait.

Forgiveness is the letting loose of that which with time will poison us.

Increase the good things, thoughts and deeds decrease the negative, bad needs.

If we seek to be light we must lose those things that tie us down tight.

All ways say we should not wait to take out those things acting as weights.

All ways say we may take away that which is our inner naysayer.

We winnow, sift and separate as if to lift the dirty window.

We seek to master the self by relinquishing to attain real joy.

We fools still become pack mules with backs laden to try climb a steep hill.

We should let go that yet that no longer gets us where we want to go.

Exploration of dark self may purify better than containment.

Purification is ridding of what does not serve for the future.

Away from discord to accord is a way away from false self.

Blake corroded his copperplates away to make the true words shine out.

There's no need to be saintly or perfect or flawless or non-carnal.

Simplicity and humility release us rather than burden.

Purge, not to be miserable but to forge the container for bliss.

Kenosis was the name for emptying to receive the flow for some.

Clarify by avoiding distortion and generalisation.

Not sackcloth, ashes but as in art purify to make more intense.

If I die id-identified not ib, I'd defy the deity.

Through opaque quest for opal rest we must cleanse the lens of perception.

There may be a catharsis, a process of polishing perfection.

The flail of the gods was a symbol of ridding and harvesting.

Washing of the heart and mind has been a way to the original.

The firing of the mind and heart is an alchemical symbol.

If you are fired you are let go, let go ire, out of mire.

Mistakes happen, let regrets go, rectify the rectifiable.

Seek acclaim without reason then prepare yourself to maim and treason.

In your body negative feelings hide, find them and where they reside.

If unwelcome traits you can distinguish, focus, seek to extinguish.

You wrongly invest attention and let traitors in who cause tension.

Growing requires pruning. Purification means removing waste.

Some weeds are more easily plucked when fully grown, the time becomes right.

To surrender to spirit is to remove negative, keep essence.

From the ore of total consciousness we seek the core of the spirit.

Sublimate the self up to its higher being subliminally.

Fix your focus on feelings of charity and humility.

Pain occurs to the self if we seek wrong. Let go and go the right way.

You fill all your senses to the brim but lose vim. Create space to grow.

Be still, to distill the essence in silence, attune lips to the heart.

Purify your concepts, reduce, concentrate, shed even the highest.

Purest of all is so pure its essence is that it is not at all.

Purify the mind, psyche by releasing ego attachment.

The quicker the impurities are removed, the quicker the opening.

If you think honesty is not a hard taskmaster compare lying.

We do not have to retreat, withdraw from loved ones or run away.

Ego can become a monster that gravitates towards other monsters.

We may slay or rather tame ego and simplify our main frame.

Ego brittle is the plaything of your presumed self and predators.

Undue fear is the rot of what you should be, feed it or your dreams.

Dispatch that which is not part of your true self and merely negative.

Consideration and cosy contemplation can distill the soul.

Egoist, egotist, egocentric is not the end to go to.

Ego dissolves, self liberates, align goals with enthusiasm.

Let go of regret and shame as feedback loops on a spiral of growth.

Abandon states we do not want, to focus on what ideals ought to be.

2.5   Release

If we release that which is false then we allow peace forever fall.

As we reap what we there sow, that which is false and tare we must let go.

Keep the ball underwater with will, it will emerge before you still.

Be better, not bitter. Mature and eat the orange when it is ripe.

Forgiveness is a forgoing of negativity and its weight.

Release of negative emotions is first for you and then for them.

Relieve yourself of that you grieve, re-wire your model to your end.

Internal becomes infernal without inflation of the inner.

Banish guilt after you have learnt or apologised or made amends.

That you were a robber, a thug or a mug does not preclude growth.

Discard, accept the truth, existence not denying reality.

You did things before and said things that you will not do in the future.

Accept, affirm and release the negative, useless, wrong, misguided.

Aim at whatever evensong enthrals to ease the day's upheavals.

The self is a palimpsest which we scrape back keeping what is just us.

Clear the imprints, programs, scripts that do not work so you can re-emerge.

Imperil not the imperium of your soul for impish people.

Even the impossible cedes its power to imagination.

Aim to recognise the projections that serve no constructive purpose.

Aim to discover, reflect, realise, actualise future self.

Lie down and visualise yourself being lightened of past concerns.

Contemplate your self being cleansed of negative cords and thorns, brush off.

Simply tend not or imply impending terrors with your attention.

See your body surrounded by fields that ward off negativity.

If teachers appear that is fine but we teach ourself and are prompted.

Persephone and Demeter go the sacred way integrating.

Weave your dreams with imperishable seams by whatever means.

The objective is not to be perfect or perfectly remote.

Invest not in imagining on others imagining of you.

Don't allow me leave the ivy of ego the rose of self stymie.

If someone's acts persist to vex, you yourself have imposed the hex.

Scoundrels in the scandals may become the saintly ones in the sandals.

Your doubt, fear and guilt need your attention to survive, so starve them.

By abandoning one may find the real, remaining, resilient.

Reconciliation of opposites, embraced produces balance.

Spirit is to us impetus, impelling the important trips.

Impale not your personality on the stake of expectation.

Lumbered you liberate by letting the reins of wrong direction free.

Lance the boil that causes turmoil, then assoil and look for the shook foil.

Leave the stopping by others, the eavesdropping on the cackle of fools.

Let go of fear, worry, doubt, guilt, obsession and vanquish them.

Letting go allows higher power to reveal itself and unfold.

Letting go may allow recovery, recuperation, repair.

Chapter 3

True Self

3.1 Seek

Philosophers who loved wisdom once have become butchers of beauty.

They take apart meaning so it can not be put together again.

They say there is no self and so therefore there is not any true self.

They say that true self is a fiction just a clever trick of diction.

They may say there is a subject instead of a self because it fits.

Subjects may be better because Queen's subjects can be subjected.

Still there must always be the one in you which is still you through and true.

Even in NDE's there is always an I with a centre in.

The me which cannot more be pared or split is the true self within it.

Kierkegaard said the will to true self was the opposite of despair.

The I then that can fly in the sky is my nature and destiny.

True self is your lighthouse there through thick and thin to guide you safely in.

True self or self clearly integrated is individuated.

True self is necessary realm of unconditional self love.

True self is what is left when that which can be discarded is let go.

True self soon is imago, the butterfly emerging from cocoon.

True self is the essence of you sublimated to sense of sublime.

True self evolves on the way forward and allows the movement onwards.

It is due residue of us, as all false, superfluous reduce.

It is the imperturbability from full alignment of me.

True self is return to the pure stream that flowed in our being before.

True self is the harvest of investment in knowing yourself best.

True self is living in accord with the best, barest essence of us.

That which is That is immiscible if ground is found behind layers.

It recovers our past path and finds the future but masters the now.

Meekness meant a 'true knowing and feeling of a man's self as he is.'

Thus the unknown author of The Cloud of Unknowing defined it.

It is thus no surprise then that the meek shall inherit the earth.

Beg not the aegis of ego be gone but egest, egress excess.

The supreme me is super, sovereign, supercoil, superaltar.

True self may also then be no self, perhaps through self, clear as water.

It may be tathagatha to some or the approaching of that gate.

It is balanced qualities of purification and acceptance.

True self realised realises it lacks nothing and is complete.

True self then is like a diamond sphere here wholly impenetrable.

True self relaxes in reality and becomes more effortless.

True self is the emergence into light, being born, delivery.

Refining inner world allows re-focus of wasted energy.

They who are self-actualised find their true self, maybe in action.

But true self is awareness and that is more being before doing.

Movement may be the way that pays for they who do and can use body.

Wisdom, sapience flows with the currents of self-clarification.

With seeing off the unwelcome we can seek the pearlescent way.

Amber-golden heart oozes, hardens immobilising intruders.

The true self describes the self from which nothing can be taken away.

True self is essence. The essence is your spirit. The rest is false self.

Van Gogh's Potato Eaters, Beethoven's Eroica Symphony.

The gap between false self and true self is the chasm for craziness.

Interior, ulterior not exterior, inferior.

Individual, the indivisible in the invisible.

Intention in inner us is power thus sent to change worlds

Lucky is she who finds self corresponds with essence without effort.

Charisma is the face of the true self, when confusion is burnt off.

Charisma has chrism as may be chrysalis over the chasm.

True self is the true ego, the real I am, I in I, real yourself.

The interest of inscape makes 'instress' to sustain it without dress.

Be authentic. Authentic comes from 'autos' the Greek word for self.

True self is a vessel for higher forces and not a mere vassal.

Your true self is a divine spark that can ignite and cause a fire.

Your true self is the only thing you have in the end, so tend to it.

Your true self is the atom to the molecule, a basic shape.

Atom, Adam, Adamah, Aton. Beyond then the automaton.

True self is the clearest, most potent concentration of your being.

True self is left after alkahest of examination occurs.

You must here remove implanted voices not your own to hear your own.

Temptation is the test of the traveller in convincing disguise.

You must first discover, your own voice before you integrate others.

We have masks and then forget the reality that lies behind.

Shake and sift sand and see the shards of gold that remain.

Heart must become unfrozen, warmed, grow to avoid spell of ego.

The true self is wise and a source of innate wisdom to use with work.

The un-encumbered self can fly when we work well to un-tether it.

Relinquish the negative of your composition that can vanquish.

Self, concentric rings of relationships you are responsible for.

Self-purification helps you find yourself and then you help others.

The whole self recognises its darkness, purifies and discards.

True self is camouflaged in its whole nature until it arises.

The spirit of true self rises up from the ashes of illusion.

Phoenix of your essence emerges from the heat of the great seeking.

The philosopher's stone is available for the great, clearing work.

The sun, the lion, the emergent light means you walk tall and straight.

The true self will find balance easier listening with inner ear.

The search does not have to end up in a limp, wimp of neutrality.

True self is not no self, oblivion, know and grow yourself, real self.

Seek true self, get out of your way, let it act, let it act well, it will.

3.2 Serving

The spirit and its evolution involves a fierce focus on self.

Bettering self is not selfish, battering self is not unselfish.

We must tend and serve our inner flame so we can spread it further on.

If you serve vices they are your master on the road to disaster.

Mystical seeking is not sorcery for the self or by the self.

Our best cannot be seen without working with what we have been blessed.

True self renounced by ego blind will leave tragedy behind.

Service on its own is not special, for a tyrant is of no good.

Giving is spiritual when no gain nor shame is the central aim.

Giving up lets us know that by letting go it was not that we seek.

The true self emerges from a cocoon of previous incarnation.

Your true self is real fortune if you create good fortune to attune.

Doubt is a demon, but vulnerability is part of the whole.

Resentment is a trailing anchor that soon stops progression of self.

Don't let people trigger, hook, provoke, needle, imprison attention.

Serve yourself but do not sever so you can serve yourself to others.

Ultimate selfish ego-driven focus is not the way here.

You must obey soul's dictates, respect others, suspect authority.

Right the runes of your destiny ere destiny writes ruin for you.

If you should die, what is your essence? What was it? What could it then be?

The self is a rose whose blooming signifies the opening soul.

Sophrosyne could be in sound soft rose sign. Resurrection and the rose.

Empathy to others comes from experience of it to yourself.

Paradoxical focus on self and knowledge helps escape therefrom.

Awareness, consciousness is expanding, expressive above senses.

Healing is integrative and clarificatory not obscure.

Without compassion as compass within, we get lost in labyrinth.

Personality is the theatre not the essence of the self.

Ego is not gone but goes to its proper role as part of the whole.

The true self allows mystic power that then becomes activated.

We serve when we can project properly deriving new figures then.

3.3   True Self Begins to Align

As we grow in self to be true we advance to the old as the new.

Light imbued, wisdom accrued, soul food, expansive mood, seek altitude.

Attitude to advance, urge to surge, presentiment to presentment.

Be patient, kind and forgiving to yourself while learning and growing.

Aware you do not care nor sprint to stamp footprints on the map of man.

Growth is an ascending spiral we take, finding our wizard within.

Getting to know yourself involves many lessons, experiences.

Good relations on their own are not a substitute for having grown.

Get out of the way of your true self so you can link to the higher.

Reach each day for that which is the whistling branch of you, ungrasping.

Lonely selfhood path isn't isolation of ego-centrism.

The earth is the source of growth and connecting with it is crucial.

Immersion and going into water connect to the subconscious.

Create your own compassionate self, avoid and contest negative.

Your true self should never be submerged in any other identity.

Spirit is a swarm of bees that pollinate thoughts planted in the mind.

Bees of spirit make honey from your old failings, weaknesses and sins.

The feeling of growth is more important than that of error, regret.

Calmly observe, tranquil in thought, focus, lose fear and terror.

True martial artists may learn the way if their heart is pure and open.

Seek the imprint of yourself that is purest and highest reflection.

Model higher attained people as same as you as you walk the path.

Reflect in on your life and configuration and then reflect out.

The journey inside is the exploration of self and facilitation of emergence.

No other person has control over your true self, so cherish it.

If your superficial self has created a straitjacket, get out.

If you can see true self you can hitch to the wagon of intention.

Respect yourself and create the feeling of meaningful desire.

As your true self emerges, your bliss, gifts reveal what you can share.

I am a maze in a maze made aware then amazed beyond care.

Mazda, mazard, maze, wisdom in the head, azan and ayurveda.

Seek accord with your self and then you will be reconciled to others.

True self then can be refined into a finer version of itself.

The true self will have a strong sense of what is right and wrong within it.

Self clarified can align with higher beings that have the highest.

True self stripped gravitates towards its destiny, that is its trip.

Development of true self is one of continual improvement.

Finding true self may be the end of the exploration for many.

This search is the garden of remembrance, centre of deep circles.

If there we have excavated the ground, foundations can be laid.

No satire but move the satyr to satyagraha and satori.

Nothing you need is in the gift of others but the seed lies within.

We have modes and models of meaning that we can adapt, change, improve.

True self is quintessence that renders one humble or poor in spirit.

True self is a balanced composition of the fabric of being.

Incandescence reveals and emerges from the essence of space.

Rejuvenescent, pearlescent, iridescent, luminescent.

Tree rings are the history but the present bark is its armour.

Finding true self may be the end for many and allow mystic space.

Essence of self condensed creates space for the natural magic.

Self restrained but true allows celestial light stained glass go through.

Compressed with our essential there, we open forces of higher air.

Thus we searched for the bull, footprints, found it, caught it, tamed it, rode it home.

That was the first six steps of the thousand year old Ten Bulls way in Zen.

Chapter 4

Journey in Space

4.1 Quest for Meaning

True self acts of its own accord and will then move appropriately.

True self sublimated makes many possibilities for new form.

Made light, tending towards light seeking out the end speed and nature of it.

We endeavour our bonds to sever to rise ever without tether.

It never ends no matter where we will live there we tend to it still.

"and wheresoever thou mayest be, thou art a stranger and a pilgrim."

Descended into matter, mated, mixed the trick is to extricate.

Energy equals our mass there by the light in and by the light out.

Journey may be to selfhood or once found onwards or upwards from there.

We must engage in the gathering in of our meanings and inklings.

We master matter and mostly must master the mast of our bodies.

To ourselves we must compassion first show before we manifest it.

Like water, awareness is destined to move, not stagnate nor be still.

As the shaman may do or have done, the voyage is part of the ascent.

Passage in life ends in death, prepare by imagining your last breath.

Hero resides near in all and they become so when from here they go.

The wand is in the wandering, wondering, wending and winding to truth.

The route we face home is not one rooted in a place that we here own.

In spirit all are a transient, nomad, vagabond, migrant.

Call the destination peace of mind, meaning, truth, or the absolute.

Exitus, reditus, circulatio and regiratio.

Lectio, meditatio, contemplatio and transitus.

Pursuing dharma may solve the self's riddle or be the way onward.

As we have come forgetting to this place so shall we retrace the path.

Samsara comes from the Sanskrit to go round, passing through, wandering.

Safe is the ship in dock but to remain there its purpose would mock.

Sent meant to go or to feel, assent that you are sent to go and feel.

Self concentrates, the pilgrimage has been realised in parallel.

Selfhood is a spiral rising above itself, sometimes the same view.

Spiral ziggurat you ascend, inner wall fixed, steps narrow, drop near.

Spiral means that we pass by lines of connection at different levels.

We seek to confirm our discovered self and our role emergent.

Venture is a spirit rooting to true self fruiting not route away.

Inner powers unsheathed, direction is needed to express self.

The quest is most likely neither purely in or out but both at once.

The quest is a zest for vision and meaning and for connection.

They call a psychedelic experience a 'trip,' do it yourself.

The only choice when stuck in a maze is to move, hopefully with thread.

Exploring the self and true self means movement and openness to grow.

Going to the door to self creates the vehicle to travel more.

Ancient Egyptian hieroglyphics describe the mystical journey.

If I identify with genuine good then the pole draws, pollen.

Enchanted, mesmerised by the world of illusion many stay put.

Many stay because the captains of vessels will not lose their custom.

Chose to stay, sit and see the shadows in the cave to become a shade.

You unready to jaunt instead yourself or place begin to haunt.

You may not realise that you have started to move but embark.

You may not have courage to take the course, of course it may then take you.

You don't have to leave your actual home but actually leave dwelling.

You burn like a meteor, a shooting star to earth, essence remains.

Sometimes set sail, get on the rail, forget the mail, leave jail, find the grail.

A venture may be thrust upon you suddenly or eagerly sought.

The expedition must be undertaken, sometimes boats must be burned.

Meanings of itinerary unfold with obstacles turned into stepping stones.

The greatest crossing may then occur when one sits still without a stir.

Go out, set off, find your track, don't look back, cast off the skin you lived in.

Walk in the woods, you begin to sense deer before you see, smell, hear it.

You may find a silver key to transport to your own inner child.

Yourself in a strange land, a desert island, normal rules don't apply.

Myths and stories represent many patterns of spiritual growth.

Coral reef, mountain, forest, desert, tundra, ice-field, jungle, city.

Without change and movement within, you cannot move on or move others.

A progress requires that you move on, leave places behind, move up.

The great odyssey does not mean that you must leave where you are in the world.

Boats were formed from trees, the fixed thing transformed to the magic transport.

Abba, ba, baba, barco, barque, arco, arc, arcana, ark, arch, archer.

Reflecting on the golden bough in the sacred wood gave much insight.

Rock-a-bye baby on the tree tall, when then bough breaks the baby will…

Helpers always appear but nobody makes a wandering for you.

The wayfarer moves beyond 'either' or 'or' to paradox and doubt.

Peregrination is the cleansing of the doors of perception, let it go.

Beauty is a signpost on the road of evolution of spirit.

Enjoy, explore, expand whether in cloister, cell, cabin or classroom.

The evolution of spirit requires an outing through inspace.

Meaning is meant as an end to mend and not meant as means to an end.

The quest is to locate the true self through exploration, reduction.

We keep on our path of growth and not be lost for fear or entrapment.

Look for path revealed in empathy concealed and not pathology.

Roaming is within and you must go beyond the 'Here be Dragons' sign.

Enlightenment without inner journey is difficult to conceive.

Those who wish to hypnotise and use will seek to tire and confuse.

Be not open to the ruse of raising you ire to be used.

Our mission involves avoidance of scuttling our true self for froth.

Our inner trek is path, hill, ladder, voyage, carpet, chariot.

Our lives uses spirals allowing us to pass points at different levels.

'Scent of the Rose-Garden reached thee and thou didst go to the Rose-Garden.'

4.2   Living in a Material World

We must make us master of our existing material make-up.

Whatever physical us, marvellous start for spiritual art.

We are meant to master our flesh fairly and not to thrash nor thresh it.

We are in carnal form and at the carnival celebrate it.

We seek to manifest manifold energies of the manifold.

Walking is the gift of the way of our ancestors or creators.

We wish to have physical body, mind and spirit come in accord.

The right internal path is not an easy one in the external.

The description of a journey is not to be the journey itself.

The mountain is as temple in body, mountain touches the sky.

The lessons are inscribed in all things bright and beautiful or ugly.

On the way we must stop and stare at lessons awaiting everywhere.

Try to see the yellow lotus in muddy water, the sunflower.

Be wise as serpents, but keenly aware of them, inside and outside.

Sift your senses to shift your attention to the expansive, the swift.

Embodied consciousness denies not but celebrates our bodies.

Body must be respected as a fractal of great intelligence.

Inversion, hands on ground, makes energy flow the other way round.

Vortex is vehicle and form and signature of the universe.

You are in a sea of suggestion with strong undercurrents and storms.

Your inner self is not a wilderness to examine from a ledge.

You may drift, driven at times but always lift your eyes with your gifts.

If not captain of ship of soul, don't complain about destination.

If currents of your heart carry you rapidly or into doldrums, adapt.

After earning and learning fore and aft, you manage and steer the craft.

Meaningful intention, purpose, objectives clarify direction.

We seek to be master of our bodies not slaves to our passions.

The material reality must be dealt with and understood.

The method of dealing with the material world we must then know.

While we must master the material we cannot just trust in dust.

Materialism is not sole matter, mother of our thinking.

Consciousness makes material reality manifest to us.

Consciousness is not only that tale told and sold by materialists.

Let not your mind be trapped in a cage of materialist tales.

You are not selfish gene in a hole, clever monkey without soul.

4.3   Inspace Seeking

Uccello's Hunt in the Forest may seek to show thoughts futile search.

The turning in of the light of consciousness has always been a way.

The connection with the intention, focus and awareness makes it.

Sediment of false self once allowed to settle creates clarity.

You look within, you seek to know and understand while watching yourself.

You go in with your own trance and control, change and heal naturally.

Inside you, your nature is your natural ally, naturally.

Inly, innings, innate, inwards, inholding, intrinsic, innards.

Interior of us is beyond the inn of outward involvement.

Inklings in us linking, sinking and lining within the king of us.

Your inside, inspired, inner being, being you is the spirit.

If in spite of this, spirit is a pit, then accept inner being.

If heart is open, movement make many open to higher perception.

The external is managed by adapting, framing and re-framing.

Within is hidden the stone, matter spirally transmutes to spirit.

Create a path through space for the soul to transit now and thereafter.

The soul needs space to expand the iteration of its own essence.

Going underground and sinking, down the steps, descending, not thinking.

Travel like an hypnotic induction, below, down under to trance.

Sibilant susurrations and the mind cedes, the illusion recedes.

Seeds sprout, the out recedes, surceases so sleep allows spirit settle.

Space is made when emptiness or gaps are perceived and heart is open.

Swallows by religion become battery hens not allowed to go.

Use words to re-position yourself so you can escape from non-words.

Empty the cup, leave it there to the end and regrets will vanish.

Create each day space for joy, exhilaration, exploration, play.

Epiphanies that happen make you happy have had pain.

Be yourself unmediated and meditate to be better.

Parallax proves that position pre-dictates and predicates, so move.

The capoeirista slave playing was freer than the slavemaster.

Creation of physical and mental space facilitates whole space.

We inform by bringing proper form in to model true reality.

Find out what inheres, what is in here, what lies herein. The inherent.

You inherit the inherent, partly divine, lesser. Distinguish.

You look in, you travel, you change, you transform, you come back.

Life is about constant growth and if not internal is tragedy.

Stay away from those who vampirise energy, use you to their end.

Synchronicities may corroborate patterns hoisted upon us.

Self in universe on right path, right spirit advances its traverse.

Oranges and lemons say the bells . . trap well the sound sense repeated.

Feeling is not about casting a net of shame, blame, guilt or doubt.

Many people love their problems and refuse to let go and move on.

In the wrong state, recognise, re-calibrate and shift to better.

Intelligibility of subtler planes of the planet come.

Flow states come to those in action who know what they do and know themselves.

Too much knowledge and not enough feeling might paralyse the will.

To find the crown as a habit whole, go in, go down the rabbit hole.

To pray is to punctuate the illusion of confinement of mind.

There is no way, many ways, the way must be shown and cannot be said.

This might be seen as the riding of the bull home stage in some thinking.

Chapter 5

Invisible Sight

5.1 Illusion on our Odyssey

Our spiritual journey involves us in the unfamiliar.

We forgo seeing for the familiar of the familiar.

We forge a constant delusion that the present is permanent.

We forget from illusion that these lives are vanishing before our very eyes.

We perceive and apperceive through the sieve of senses and brain.

We operate, peer, engage in the world as it appears, we show up.

We may learn to see but really feel fields and sense energies unseen.

We cannot see the empty space within mass nor the air we breathe.

When we come out, come forth, enter the arena, expose, we can grow.

What you take out of the world is never visible nor portable.

Presence, phantom, phantasm, phantasmagoria, phenomenon.

The world is not what it appears, what doesn't appear is critical.

The apparent world is not the totality of reality.

The apparent, sensible and visible may be something else.

The intangible, unknown is more active than many can perceive.

The imperceptible dimension of mind and spirit must prevail.

Occult meant that which is hidden. Mysticism from word to conceal.

Matters in immaterial realms matter reams more than what seems.

Seers aware see that that is not there, through that that seems to be there.

Secrets and secret conduct hides much material reality.

Reels and nets capture fish, in reality nets you are caught too.

Visible world is an over-simplified version of existence.

Our focus on visibility can limit knowability.

Visibility is mutable, a mere shadow of perception.

Ignorance is not just not knowing but also implies not seeing.

Pattern, synchronicities may indicate other realities.

Knowing the frontier of visible and invisible is wisdom.

Much energy is invisible in universe of energy.

Baseless fabric of material yields to other reality.

Simple consciousness mistakes physical matter for all that matters.

The eye is easily confused and deceived even when it sees.

The ear can often experience more, find balance open the heart.

Ninjas and robbers are quiet, not all that is serene is wanted.

People's souls are not transparent nor visible and we forget this.

Seek clear contemplation to find concord for complex sense of seeing.

Vision of the sweat lodge is the mindset of another dimension.

We are carried on waves, make waves, go through waves, change waves unseen.

We should not seek the genie but discover the genius in us.

We are hypnotised in an illusion within a butterfly's dream.

We must behold lest we play blindman's buff in the cold with the beasts.

5.2 Prey

The towel with the most complex pattern distracts and hides the most dirt.

The trowel may help the builder build and bury the unwanted things.

Limited in what we see outside and inside we are easy prey.

Malevolence manifests and exists and must be considered.

The predator sneaks up on prey and does not forewarn, so we ready.

Secret in the open is a fish out of water. Are you in it?

Invisibility allows priesthoods control prey and prayer.

Conspiracy is done in secret concertation for control.

We become drunken monkeys with bums to the temple to beg for nuts.

We live in a reality show with the conceit that we produce it.

Religion can produce an illusion of that which it promises.

Amassing of masses run by elites to master spirit must miss.

Priesthoods may have benefits but cannot be substitutes for growth.

Arch, archon, archetype. Go your own way whole, without losing control.

Dogma dogs many, may do harm to spirit without experience.

Dogma, feeling unmatched, hatches hatchet-men in its hatchery.

Does your conception of God really hinder your spiritual growth?

Energies, entities feel entitled to fall in etheric field.

You, a child of the universe must check the chill of ill will sent.

A great architect may take a bad commission for a bad building.

Sacrifice is not sacerdotal but sacred sadhana may show.

Do not open or relinquish your soul to others here or yonder.

Beware those who say you have no spirit or assume control of it.

Patternicity, paranoia will be used against all seekers.

Vulnerable, gullible and ill people must be extra careful.

5.3 Vision

Lo and behold the gold you were told of old is not to be sold.

It's not appearance that matters but appearance of inner power.

Imagine where and what you want and feel it, make-believe, realise.

In Dante's view, blessedness rests first on vision and then love follows.

If we cultivate insight we render invisible seeable.

Ignorance is not just to see what is there as well as not to know.

The undiscovered continent within is the one we should see best.

The inner eye sees deeper, further over time through past and future.

The body has more potential sites of sight than merely the eyes.

The vision needed is to be able to see whole and see the whole.

To see through is the most potent power that you can grow and nourish.

See with clear eyes, see through, see beyond, see it as it is, see soundly.

Seeing with heart's eyes the real world is the art of living whole and true.

We can transform our seeing, our perception and our reality.

What is wrong with wondering whether you can see something far away?

Bigger vision leads to inner eye, third eye, lantern of Osiris.

Practice the action of the inner eye to see without refraction.

As the ego diminishes the scales should fall from the eyes. Insight.

All ancient wisdom had a comprehension of invisible force.

Chi, prana, manitou, ruah, mana, maban, baraka, vital force.

Hear, hark and listen. The ear must work with the eye in darkness and light.

You can see with your 'second brain,' feel with guts, harken to your 'hara.'

Visualise, envisage, have vision, that is the most potent sight.

Create a valuable vision you pursue, innovate and effect.

Like the wind, move the thing waiting to be moved with invisible forces.

Vision quest has always been to help you and others on the right path.

Some selves may become seers through looking deeply within and without.

Ancient cave-painters left abstract marks probably from inside them.

Alphabet of universal symbols perceptible to all them.

Universal grammar or language instinct exist, spirit moreso.

In visions you can move and partake but not if you hallucinate.

Transcendental vision is not of eye or mental made but higher.

If you use magic beans to make a stalk you will have to slay giants.

In different dimensions we must then see and detect differently.

On the electromagnetic spectrum we can see but a sliver.

We delude ourselves to think we can see all there is to be seen.

Then we take our small field of vision and fill it up with a screen.

A screen is something to keep other stuff out, so don't you be in doubt.

A Fata Morgana, the Flying Dutchman are seen with outer eye.

The mighty lens within lends light so we can see another world.

The mystical is the optical of spiritual consciousness.

Without reflection, refraction or perception there are no rainbows.

Chapter 6

Knowing Not

6.1 Knowing no Wisdom

We must avoid mistakes of thought to our destination to be brought.

The passage of spirit must not be trapped in a sensible mirage.

Your vehicle, transport of meaning is made from knowledge and truth.

Steering between the Scylla and Charybdis of knowing and not.

The cloud of forgetting is part of the way to mystical accord.

If we can learn to forget, let go of knowing we can feel higher.

Before we forget, we must learn how to operate in this time and space.

Distinguish, test, evaluate, be sceptical, fight to keep truth.

Riddle, rhyme, rebus reveal rivers raking realms refill.

The absolute truth cannot be that there is no absolute truth.

Underground streams can have great force and power unseen.

We must participate with discernment in the ostensible world.

There are many who will confuse, delude and misuse you with knowledge.

What know alchemists, conjurors, quizmasters, poker-players, jokers?

Every group of people has something for the riddles and enigmas.

Be pragmatic about how you can earn and grow what you need to learn.

Supremely useful methods of truth-finding are not the supreme truth.

The parent doesn't need evidence of their instinct for it to exist.

The scientist can be bought, remote, they often rely on belief.

The scientists are not the science, their logic is not ultimate.

Comprehensibility of parts doesn't reveal meaning of the whole.

Initial unintelligibility may be new dimension.

Values, purposes and qualities are sidelined and substituted.

Sometimes scientists study something useful for unhappy reason.

The magician and the mystic share some important territory.

Great science so mysterious is but magic by another name.

Numbers, symbols, patterns, shapes, growth and form militate against chaos.

But let go those who will project the limitations of words on you.

Many may look to stunt your growth to seek you stay where they are stuck.

In your journey, what is wise and true may be hidden or occulted.

One of the secrets hard to see, that everyone can a mystic be.

Emerald, jade, forest heart made from energy not to feel nor fade.

Green wind, green wheel, green branches, green man, green hills in the verdant world.

When war is justifiable, a slight offensive, it is upside down.

Seek some discipline of reason and also rapture of revelation.

Meaning is of mind but spirit is also feeling and experience.

6.2 Narrow Knowledge

Mind may make a real misery of a practical paradise.

Explanation may destroy the insight, truth come from experience.

Maturing is not more or less passing for us of a Turing Test.

Philosophy was a love of wisdom that perished into debate.

Creativity is a wild mountain goat that has been put in a pen.

Spiritual matters are often bigger than the sum of their parts.

Some things can be taken apart but not put back together again.

Knowledge is often a reduced, instant powder with missing pieces.

Education calculated to cauterise imagination.

Don't waste energy trying to convince those who will imprison you.

Logic, analysis, philosophy can be virus to being.

The empire of empiricism has had many pyrrhic victories.

The study of the spirit and consciousness is still empirical.

Filled with facts we are still ignorant and often deluded.

One fact may be true but the world works in combinations of facts.

Science without conscience is then a con doctrine of domination.

Science seeks to know the inner being to control it not to aid.

Behind the cold sense of science are wizards of war without pity.

Science can't require evidence while experience is denied.

Science is useful, but the bastard scientism is dangerous.

Evolutionary psychology is a misleading doctrine.

Not looking for proof of subtle and unseen you can't be aloof.

We can't comprehend complexity of universe rationally.

Great science often came from the impulse of those who believed in God.

Do you know the end of knowing can never be the end of knowing?

De-construction without repair re-construction is then destruction.

Jack and Jill went up the hill to fetch a pail of... What did he break?

That which is counter-rational may triumph over the rational.

The rational trumps authority but the rational is rationed.

The cat is good at climbing up trees but not so good at coming down.

Topaz light touches the tender heart that expands the scope of knowing.

Context that comes from Latin root 'to weave.' One thread does not make a mat.

All great spiritual texts have spirit in them sometimes obscured.

What if yet another ancient pot was unearthed in the desert?

Let not your life and your spirit be condemned to be condensed.

You choose to use the losing of life-power potion imposed or not.

Undue pride of knowing, on a rodeo ride you will be going.

Being poor in spirit was good, implying humble inner mind.

In Buddhism, humility creates emptiness from the false.

Better to know a little that is right than a lot that is wrong.

Thus we should know the limitations and illusion of knowledge.

We can learn from those who learnt so we can earn the truth we have yearned.

In Taoism, they know that it is good to know that you do not know.

Better to be a fool unknowing if you knew eternal rules.

The true self on mystic routes learns, knows, perceives and receives truths.

Chapter 7

Nature of Knowing

7.1 Body

True self masters the body to go, come into accord and to know.

The body developed whole with spirit is path to the higher things.

We tenderly tend to body bond not the end but base for beyond.

It is not that we relegate fleshy form but we delegate it.

It is not that we don't love life but seek the eternal supernal.

The flesh serves the spirit for its cherished form shall deserve to perish.

Within the body are smaller bodies and larger bodies without.

We must tend to our body with light, cold, heat, green, sun, water and wind.

Carnal cathedrals of spirit are holy place of sanctuary.

We keep whole healthy the holy of holies having to approach.

Sacrum rooted in the word sacred like sacrament with mystery.

Body and life is sacred cared and we dare and should not be scared.

Lie down on your back let out sigh as if to death, reflect and die.

In the body be calmly based never regard it with distaste.

To despise the body is odd and nowise wise in the eyes of mind.

We wear our false self down to our awareness of our awareness.

Smooth the stone worn by dripping of the softest thing incessantly.

We have many senses inside, much more than Aristotle told us.

There are bodies in bodies, separable for those who believe it.

Spirit journey begins in body, but it is not destination.

Body is a temple reflecting a higher that creates temples.

As the placebo shows, body has power if it activates it.

Above the cathedral entrance is the tympanum, pass through the ear.

Use body to climb the ladder wise, like honey hunters after prize.

Do not become martyrs or sacrifices for others' games.

The body can know that which the mind cannot perceive or understand.

Attend the 'hara,' the gut, the dantian and let not sorrow mend.

To some Virgo here and the nerves, instinct, sense, being inside person.

Feminine energy within material to unfold, unite.

Our body can learn, feel and sense subtle vibrations and energy.

Care of the body facilitates flow of spirit influx, inflow.

Be comfortable in your body, ignore others controlling views.

Wit is with you always to please the body, desire to master.

Pain may provide the potential to activate the need to know.

Body must be cared for as whole entity with flows of energy.

Yoga may be the right path if spirit is conscious of objective.

Altered states, senses in heat, cold, wood, hill, water, air, rhythm, dance, trance.

Adopt, adapt to accommodate the appearance to become adept.

Senses keep us alive and the spirit vessels working intact.

Movement is a path to all the higher elements on the right way.

The world we perceive is not really transparent and truth is obscure.

Plants have intelligences that can tell things to the human body.

We can approximate but not know insensible with sensible.

Understand reality, make real, bring it into reality.

Cipher, decipher, cycle, disciple, cypress, decryption, crypt.

7.2   Accord

The word 'accord' (agree, correspond) comes from the Latin 'to the heart.'

Accord can be an agreement, harmonious union, covenant.

We usually accord respect to others, agree or reconcile.

We seek accord with the greatest of teachers though they be a handful.

At the core within, to be in accord and then without and above.

Accord may be in the vibrations in sound in wavelengths in breathing.

If you do something of your own accord it is voluntarily.

The more that some perceive is the core of us and of all that exists.

Discord, disharmony- a spiral staircase to negativity.

Create an accord of awareness with your awareness as ground.

Mind should dissolve at times into heart until it is automatic.

Some describe the accord as vibrational between yourself, others.

With then the tincture of your instinct you can cure your thinking within.

Be as cordial as you can to begin with all and work from there.

Allow a sphere to grow from a point of clarity in your heart.

Pythagoras saw the cord, monochord and chords. Music of spheres.

Some see a core of practices among shamans across history.

Capoeira berimbau, cord from ancestors, through heart to circle.

Through thick and thin ever in balance, accord un-fixed, dynamic dance.

Knowledge without being in accordance with awareness is no sense.

It is not just what we know with the intellect but more in the heart.

Learn to listen and you will be able to resonate with the sound.

We must seek accord with our beliefs, feelings, goals and intentions.

Elucidation of grand strategies without focus on heart fails.

Words without experience and application are not the full story.

Courage comes from 'couer' from heart not the brain, we find it there.

That which is arrogant, controlling and cruel is not the right path.

The clear heart having chosen the correct path cannot fail whatever.

Heart is the chamber of distillation of spirit water of life.

From the spring in self is the aqueduct from heart to head to fountain.

The heart and head in accord with our own nature within and without.

Spinal cord is a channel, sushumna, tree of life, axis mundi.

There are conspiracies. The verb 'conspire' means to breathe together.

Make sure you gravitate to spirits that you want to be breathing with.

We are bound by invisible cords to others that we must watch.

Some see the silver cord connecting the soul to its sacred shell.

Learning can come on an arc from the arcanum and the archangel.

Equilibrium, Libra to some, centred, ready for what's to come.

Finding the whole, true self rightly allows access to higher realms.

Concord, in accordance with your true self and your purpose, in accord.

Marsilio Ficino sought concord to reconcile diversity.

Concord was where Emerson, Thoreau and transcendentalists lived.

The heart can foster sapientia which was a more sacred knowledge.

Seek core of gnosis steer away from avidya or ignorance.

If what you are and what you do match, the current of life you catch.

What we do when we have learnt is to accept the cloud of unknowing.

Contemplation is the full accord of our being with the sacred.

Accord allows correspondence occur answering as together.

To some there is a common core of mystical experience.

Unitive, knowledge-endowing, ineffable and self-effacing.

The mystic spiral passes the feelings before winding higher.

Mystical accord allows mystical awareness be embedded.

Mystical accord seeks to be a practice of the perennial.

Mystical accord is the lost chord that is touch of infinite calm.

7.3   Clues for Reflection

Look again at the obvious things and wonder at their mystery.

Language words literal letters numbers have meaning more than we know.

The threshold of transcendence is held short of meaning for heaven's sake.

Words house worlds hidden within them to be heard to rouse unbidden.

'Love many, trust few, always paddle you own canoe.' An old saying.

Ask if everything is inverted, subverted in our universe.

Insight from outside may emerge and agree with conscious construction.

Entangled, even in discord cause spooky action at a distance.

Language has embedded wisdom, sacred is said, word ghosts of sages.

Links at times are lucky, enlightening, logical to make you think.

Clusters of words may (or may not) betray the lustre of lost meaning.

Playing a game is not the same as seeking to aim for high wisdom.

For some it may be to 'let go and let God' to get right thinking.

Pragmatism is one useful bridge for good hearts across to good goals.

Phenomenological analysis works, why not just listen?

Tetragrammaton means four letters. Spell with letters, magic spells.

I am in the Three Forms of First Thought, hidden, coming then unbidden.

'Tragedy' comes from the Greek word for goat, catharsis has art in it.

Sometimes we need to be tricked in order to do good or to feel it.

Lux, lumen, luck, lord, Lugh, Luke, lullaby, library and liberty.

It is foolish to ignore magic because you disagree with it.

Meditate, edit time and date, mantra, art of man, manna, mate.

Plain language has hidden residues of obscure, occult significance.

The five elements theory with ether or spirit can be helpful.

Either is ether in there, there is in ether, neither here nor there.

Cathar, catharsis, charm, Charon, Charis, chakra, chan, chant, ka.

Catechism, cathexis, catheter, cataleptic, cataphysical.

Ocean surface roughish below calm, colourful fish, friendly, flashing.

Most systems with trees do teach- ash, oak, boab, bodhi, banyan and peach.

We know there is often a tree of life and forget the tree of death.

Tet, torus, tarot, tao, Torah, tor, Thor, Thoth, theta, theos, theory.

Toora loora loora, toora loor a li. Nonsense, but maybe not.

Tones recur in words that have impact. Sounds open up wheels of new worlds.

The quintessence and the sixth sense are part of the system of knowing.

Hall, halo, hallow, hallelujah, hallo, hallucinate.

Accident, suddenness, surprise, shock occasion illumination.

Brahma, Abraham, Saraswati, Sarah, Tara, Terah, just chance?

Sidhe, siddhi, Setanta, Siddharta, Kulkulkan, Cuchulainn.

Hypnosis and hypnagogia may be windows on the psyche.

Hypnosis, NLP, suggestibility because of words.

"In the beginning was the Word, and the Word was with God, and the Word.."

Grimoire, magic book, grammar, latter from the Greek the 'art of letters.'

Recognise cults, hierarchies and priesthoods for what they really are.

Geneva, genie, genius, genome, gens, gentile, genital.

You are open to outside persuasions you do not now realise.

Doubt is often an intrusion of external force to thwart heart.

Lodge, logos, log, logia, logodaeldulus, logogriph, Loki.

Boehme, shoemaker, Schumann frequency, free man, qui vive, quo vadis.

The fantasy that you pay for is a fantasy that you pay for.

Tranquility without vigilance is quality of subservience.

Ra, rabbi, ray, Rama, Rahman, Amun Ra, ram, radiate, ratio.

Tara, hara, mantra, rajah, ray, ratzon l-kabel, Raphael.

God is a cipher for complexity beyond comprehension.

Enthusiasm, entheogens are not concepts without God.

Joan of Arc, Swedenborg, Boehme, Blake, Rasputin, Yeats. Yeast for the soul?

We become vessels, structure and form with space and emptiness balanced.

Every advance begins with some jolt to yourself or bolt from the blue.

Go, good, gold, gong, God, goal, goat, goggle, gonad, gondola, gossamer.

Oscillation, duality permeates, cause and effects explains.

Chi kung, tai-chi, ju-jitsu, judo can be spiritual practice.

Glad embrace of mystery instead of existential misery.

Michael in the mystical in alchemical, acme, calm and chime.

Synthesise, syncretise, synchronise spirit experience of folk.

Do, re mi, fa, so, la, ti, do. Dyeus, ra, ma, far, soul, law, deus.

Ut, Re, Mi, Fa, Sol, La. These are the original solfeggio.

Word, world, worth, Wordsworth, wood, wa, wand, water, Watan Tanka, Wotan.

You must feel your impact on others, it will fill you without fail.

To be or not to be is not to be the answer as you will be.

9 or 7 key to some- 1, 2 , 3 or 4, but numbers open doors.

0 Origin, 1 individual, 2 expansion, 3 nurture,

4 thought, 5 exploration, 6 based, 7 reach up, 8 unity.

9 reaching down, 10 union. Extraordinary in common sight.

64 Symbols in Enochian, I Ching, Chessboard, DNA.

If spirit exists wherefrom? What is the highest? If not what is left?

Cover, coven, convert, convent, covenant, convention, convergence.

Watch how spirit skeptics question without offering any answers.

If people choose to just 'exist' perhaps they can from judgment desist.

To have lived is to see the devil backwards. Don't be bedevilled, live.

If you can, walk, it is the easy and ready wonder of the wander.

The Transcendentalist and Romantics may have got it, but you have it.

The Buddha, a buddha means one who knows, is enlightened or woke up.

Then bending the tending of women and men's shen lends zen ending.

All numbers have tales to tell and threads to follow, none are made hollow.

Seventh Heaven, Heaven Seventeen, A Clockwork Orange, orangutan.

"Wholly on heavenly things my mind is set…" Donne's Sonnet 17.

CV 17 is Sea of Tranquility acupressure point.

17 seconds is the space for Law of Attraction's optimum time.

17 is The Star Tarot card of balance and inspiration.

17th of Tammuz is an important date in Judaism.

717 is the Holy Grail story set, forwards, backwards.

1717 Grand Lodge of Freemasonry in London formed.

For 17 seconds sun shines into inner chamber of Newgrange.

Magicicada emerge every 17 years in transforming.

Genesis 17 is the covenant with aged Abraham.

About 17% who clinically die have NDEs.

17 rare earth elements are there not spare but significant.

Sutra in haiku for form's sake suits sources as mosaic of meaning.

7.4   Sources

The greatest source is described as 'The Source' by many other people.

Some see us as the wave breaking from a cosmic sea of consciousness.

Curiosity is the source of all learning and of all cures.

The accumulation of gold of spirit is the only wealth.

We learn to know through revelation, study, play and self-mastery.

There is a time for critical thinking, a time to abandon it.

Knowing can come through a range of different channels that are opened.

From turquoise twilight to blue night descends the sense of immanence.

Form in nature is a concrete echo of universal meaning.

The truth is often revealed if we commit to find it fully.

The world of the spirit has levels to balance evolution's speed.

Seeing is limited but develop your depth you can see the universe.

Symbols have potent implication through inner power, projection.

Focus on a flower find the signature of the intelligence.

Dandelion is a weed, menace to many, a miracle to some.

Compassion to one in fact is better than a million in theory.

All knowledge without self-knowledge is a tree without roots.

Much knowing, action, invention comes from the mystical realm.

Mythology is the map and territory of understanding.

Energy is life, magic, meaning, material, comprehension.

We find ourself and then open the sluices of commonality.

When worked out, the true self knows what it wants with ease and aligns.

Failure is an agent of learning, demands responsibility.

Responsibility to you, others is no burden when aligned.

Intuition becomes stronger than reason through self becoming true.

Awe and wonder we won on birth, let it not be squandered or stolen.

Understanding unravels into focus and new experience.

Unthinking into feelings sense subtle, translating experience.

Perennial philosophy fills all and any of us open.

If you examine what is mine, my world, I examine what is thine.

Pragmatic and cosmopolitan views will cohere and not confuse.

Revelation appears out of the blue without rationality.

Our knowing must become easy, ingrained, incorporated, enshrined.

Learn to learn, work, be, let go, concentrate, create, act and manifest.

The subjective is the I to be owned so origin can be known.

Chapter 8

Distraction and Attraction

8.1 Concentration

As self seeks then to stay true, spirit must journey home or away too.

If true self allows spirit be released, expansion will not be ceased.

Assign cares to sinking sediment in the mind's fish tank to see self.

If true self is attained the stickiness of attachment dwindles.

Don't waste time on other's idle fancies, fix and focus on target.

Distraction is pursuit of mirage of substance with feeling absent.

Love may be an unreal lie and just the mere appearance of it.

Change focus through concentration on meaning, don't feed negatives.

Distraction and attraction contain the word action coloured thereby.

Cultivate focus and fixity of purpose, dedicate the mind.

Consciousness living in distraction grows further from potential goals.

Concentration is a weather-vane unless we fix its direction.

Concentration is not the problem. It is lack of concentration.

Concentration has coruscating power mostly from calm mindset.

Concentration through contemplation is special way of attention.

Attention is the arrowhead of consciousness narrowing to point.

Art is a process of refinement and concentration, so spirit.

Super focus is fuel that allows vessel of being propel.

Withdraw mind's attention from objects to timeless awareness at times.

Focus on certain objects is another way to still the mind.

Pythagoras meant music and numbers to be thoroughfares to truth.

All mysticism involves powers of concentration and control.

Paradoxically abandoning attention is critical.

Stop and stare with time, without a care, at sunsets, showers and rainbows.

See the miracle in the familiar, do not project contempt.

The right conditions come when you fix them and combat distractions.

Meditation is a metaphor for mastery of distraction.

Short-cuts on a spiral of spiritual growth are dangerous.

Skip spiral in spirit you can be put in jeopardy and peril.

Bring consciousness to concert, concentration, concord, consecration.

The state of peace allows greater production and results if needed.

Make sure your self is not sold into slavery by your own mind.

Journey from self to higher planes require focus less distractions.

Tune then to the tone of the universe that vibrates in harmony.

Attend to the self, so make it true to you, minimise distraction.

You cannot get it, if your attention has been so much distracted.

Learning to cycle look to the horizon not down to the ground.

We are thralls enthralled in thrall instead of you are that, all that we are.

Concentration is bringing to a centre. I am, I am centre.

Marshal the mad monkeys in your mind so they cannot marshal you.

8.2   Diversion

Two forces pulling attention is the house divided that can't stand.

'And it is not possible for a servant to serve two masters.'

Without a flail against distractions we fail and ail, and miss the nail.

Disenchantment takes time, space from that purpose which with joy you should face.

Penny arcades of political debate will cost you preciously.

War and global politics is a racket, leave it, don't believe it.

Slot machines of public affections drain a lot from your life force.

Lost in the mire of will o' wisps, dwelling with wisdom seems amiss.

No pockets in shrouds, no popularity contests in clouds beyond.

When you are being cheered in the arena look out for the lions.

Self-deception is a distraction made dangerous by denial.

We tell tall tales to ourselves wholesale entailing then dissipation.

Groups decided to rob people of their mystical right and rites.

Amused, bemused passively, used instead of using creative muse.

Pale substitutes prevent attention and mystic participation.

Imagine some doubts, fears are imps you were unaware you must manage.

Theatre from the Greek word to 'behold' or 'see.' Learn to see instead.

Put the VR halter on your head, you can anywhere be led.

Glamour and glamours are empty illusions often wielded for woe.

Attention facilitates, allows trojan horses, viruses in.

Doubt is a demon, but vulnerability is part of the whole.

To no avail, we bewail, derail, curtail, countervail our power.

Discord (disagreement, dissonance) in Latin means apart from heart.

People find confinement in their mental world and forget the fine ones.

Hoodoo works on you if your attention is concentrated on pin.

Bullies or fools with words will prick, but only you decides what will stick.

Who does your mind dwell on? Do you want their spirit then dwelling in you?

The soul cannot be captured as easily as the body but can.

Mind may be trapped in labyrinth, fog, prison in a hall of mirrors.

The thing we think we want to attend may not be what you want to get.

Mundane is made of distraction irrelevant to reality.

The most false things are said to be reality without irony.

Diversion re-directs roads, attention, also means entertainment.

'Entertain' means to hold the attention of. What price is your attention?

TV makes you medium and product, deluded that you control.

Screens deflect your energy away from the vertex to veneers.

We have outsourced our attention and our free will will follow for free.

TV remote control isn't what you do, but what it does to you.

With the screen now you are seen too, you are then put into the new zoo.

Desire to play with reality is a false panacea.

The bared teeth of the aggressive animal is confused for a smile.

Mercenary souls cause havoc. Constant hearts move like flags in the wind.

Passive acquiescence is not a synonym for spiritual.

For some the journey after death replays avoidance of distraction.

Matter is mother not to be flattered with exclusive attention.

8.3   Susceptibility

While we wish our seeds to blossom in the field we are treated as weeds.

Vigilant we invigilate lands lately with sigils secret sown.

Attraction of 'spirits' to drink, mimics innate possibility.

Beware of use of spiritual terms to obscure meaning.

The fork in the road of truth follows on from the fork in the tongue.

Inverted use of spiritual terms betrays negative purpose.

Identity, personality is a big, distracting construct.

Too many possessions suck energy and dissipate concentration.

Distraction means 'to draw away.' From what? Distraction is dis-spiriting.

The uncommitted heart is prey to enticement by wrong direction.

Mechanical mesmerism shapes ego to ape false success.

The whole person can seek the spirit or perish in perdition.

Sin is a frail symbol for wrong direction, not mainly punishment.

Keep out of the black maria of things magic you don't understand.

Fantasy can be hitched to an unhelpful wagon going wrong ways.

Fiction, fantasy have become dull and enslaving without insight.

False enchantment is a curse without contribution to the spirit.

Instead of feeling and culture by gift and grace we get a script.

Positive cause can be attacked, maimed by predatory people.

Do not worship a priesthood which puts itself in the way of spirit.

Don't let lesser gods become higher than the highest.

If self is sacrificed to lowly energy you will become it.

Covered in mail you can be assailed if you allow thoughts be tethered.

What you worship becomes then a matter of ultimate attention.

Macbeth shows deadly, dark, disintegrating, distracting ambition.

Be robust, tough, combative, rough with those who would seek to steal your soul.

8.4   Attraction and Attention

Action follows the path of attraction or distraction as allowed.

People of action often indicated their mystical basis.

You will attract that you adjust to, pay attention to and mirror.

Let go of holding on to old branches to allow you go forward.

If some are repelled by your clarifying force, it may be a boon.

Attraction to whatever the ego wants would then be attachment.

Only things you want to be attached to are your highest ideals.

Hail the highest from wherever you hail to ensure you do not fail.

Some call it dhyana in the looking for it, observing detached.

If true self is aligned with on high then attraction is true and wise.

When you are not distracted you can focus on attraction to you.

Don't be pre-occupied with wrong issues, change the question, change a life.

Mindfulness is valuable once it is not only about the mind.

Minor worries are insignificant yet should be ignored. Don't fret.

Caught in feeling of confusion fly to another branch see it anew.

Pain can transform if it is seen as feedback loop that can re-focus.

Instead of seeking freedom avoid being a slave, be free as a bird.

Ignore the grumblings of the sleepers as they are meaningless.

Heart is part of warrior spirit not to cause war but finish it.

As your heart becomes clear build a doubt-catcher to stop thoughts interfere.

Fresh the wind, fresh the trees, sun shines over passing clouds of your trouble.

Ancient myths have more meaning than many modern manifestations.

Angels are more easily perceived and heard when we are silent.

Ancestors forgotten, unknown are in you and should be respected.

Attention is the basis of attraction and advancement.

Attend to your attention in the end then it is all you can tend.

Artists should seek to bring your attention then towards the numinous.

Consider past cares that vanished like snow in sunshine.

Non-distraction is essence of the still where essence is distilled.

Become attracted to the upper force through the narrow gate and path.

There is then verticality, there is an axis of attraction.

If you must, cannot trust, then think electromagnetic energy.

Link yourself in mind to all things or yourself become dissolved, melted.

It may be said that the bull is transcended in the Ten Bulls pictures.

Be attracted to arc encircling your heart to your beginning.

Be a suscipient to that which is in accord with your true self.

Be tinder then ready to light in there tender to divine spark.

Anger is fire of heart hearth to be contained and not consumed.

Sit in the inglenook and use that power for other broth to cook.

Worship is a ship to what we concentrate on without distraction.

Worship is a force of attraction. Be careful for what you worship.

Remember recreation is re-creation of you, so own it.

Keep clear stillness inside, let go fear, undue pride, deep truth will not hide.

Seek simplicity, spiritualise the body, harbour truth.

Oscillate from void to vaguely visualise deity or Dao.

The mystical is ethic of focus on eternal internal.

Chapter 9

Transcendence

9.1 Unify

Our original possibility is bliss and is the goal too.

The way above our self to forget illusion of limitation.

Bliss that smoulders and persists is this kiss of heaven's own solder.

All traditions of spirit suggest unitive possibility.

Our destiny is to relate which means to bring back, make relations.

Released by seed, on stem of true self, flower of spirit seeks the sun.

Sun unbeknownst had nourished ground and bud so flower should find it.

The unbeknownst is not the same as the unknown and non-existent.

The mystic is the gardener in the garden of the unbeknownst.

Reach a liminal, extraordinary state we have forgotten.

All mystical experience involves a rising above oneself.

Some see a merging of themselves with other forces of nature.

Drumbeats adumbrate and allow your dumb brute transmute into angels.

We allow superconsciousness to operate and resonate.

We suspend analysis, relax, escape to power potential.

Boldly passive, receptive, returned to childhood power we flower.

Reverie, an apology for idlers, is productivity.

Hesychasm allowed crossing of the chasm for some for a long time.

Peace of mind is a transcendence of toil, trouble, events and worry.

Altered states to healing, art, extra-sensory perception relate.

Trance is a sense transit portal from mortal rant to transcendence.

Transcendence surmounts objectivity towards subjectivity.

It moves from consciousness and subconsciousness to superconsciousness.

It moves from our intra essence to extra and super essence.

Looking within turns sense of reality inside-out, upside-down.

We transcend the bull and the self in the ancient Zen picture story.

Even if we reach but falling fail, reaching must to be of avail.

If we have tried and reached a ceiling, we have learned through that feeling.

As spirit of people has shown, the most common limits are our own.

Our lesser we have purged well and that allows the surge and the swell.

For many mystics, the transcendental is not merely a sought joy.

It is in this realm that gifts, powers, perceptions often recur.

Concomitant powers coming to mystics are not central to them.

Some may even find it by asomatic and parasomatic sense.

Then re-occur, recur, recure, the ur there in you is yours again

The mind is emptied to find the pure within or the linking of all.

You may work for it but you don't make it but discover and find it.

It is true reality not a trapdoor out of reality.

Reality and consciousness link, the deviation around us.

Some call this high realm of pure experience the trans-subjective.

Seek the true zen in the zenith through non-seeking.

The Chinese shen is in the heavens on earth and then it is in us.

We emerge from the cave through the tunnel into the bright, brave light.

Plato saw a world of ideals above the world of appearance.

Analogy, metaphor are actual things that are or may be.

From here the severe sere below coheres there the near sky revered.

Fear that inheres is left to the light that rises like a mere feather.

Fear is the feather exactly. Make fear feather you easily face.

Her feat fathered, Shakti meets Shiva, Purusha leaves Prakriti.

Feather is a symbol of inspiration to the netherworld.

Balance is between the crook of mercy and flail of severity.

Epiphanies allow a sudden finish, spinning web of meaning.

Transcendent goes beyond identity, boundary, culture, time, space.

Transcendent is the pioneer sphere beyond the mere ends of land.

Transcendent is space of the mythic and archetypal domain.

Transcendent is that which is above thoughts and a priori in us.

The mystic and the mythic are my theatres yet they still might try.

Buzz of universe can be heard in us as you open up to it.

Essential self, being, rises away from objects, mind and body.

Lower self disembarked and most of the self left behind parked.

Ere eerie thoughts cohere, conspire, your spirit adheres to higher.

The transpersonal is the field of increased human potential.

All transcendence involves principally understanding littleness.

The tree of life unites above and below where roots reflect branches.

The cloud of unknowing is apprehended after a long journey.

Gaps between the clouds or in the cloud allow glimpses of the heavens.

Satori is one name for a glimpse of higher states available.

Good, positive spirit paths seek or contemplate illumination.

Even without a Great Spirit belief, the spirit is expansive.

Steer, veer, career, volunteer to go far beyond the tall thought weir.

Consciousness is naturally and inherently transcendent if let.

At the very least the need for peace of mind and contentment beckons.

Once dull, false imaginings dissolve away openness opens up.

The heart must be pure, aura cleansed and our psychic armour donned.

Transcendence moves from beyond ordinary to the ineffable.

Perennial, individual potential is most powerful.

Altruism, compassion, sometimes occulted a pre-requisite.

Occluded the ocular, occupy occident, spiritoso.

Psychedelics may insight yield but the way is in the inner field.

The first transcendence has been surmounting illusion without and in.

We must transcend our own beliefs that limit our inner powers.

Transcendence of perception allows ascension to the crown above.

The inner eye developed allows that last inner ascent beyond.

Shakespeare left things unsaid that could not be believed after he was dead.

'This poet lies. Such heavenly touches ne'er touched earthly faces.'

The desert of Sahara once again is sahasrara, fertile.

Saraha sought enlightenment alive, sahaja, natural.

Outer self must adapt to that reality, amphibiously.

Samadhi, satori, invocation, interior inwards.

Neshamah, shaman, shamash, shemash, shamayim, samhain. Spirit link.

A Ah Sha Sa Ma Ha, human, mandala, ma, asah shamah.

The wise, worked, subtle will rise till such meets in sky power falling.

As the artist creates art, create the celestial dimension.

Essential self creates the manifestation of celestial.

Terrestrial and celestial are essentially united.

Having journeyed, been self-actualised you get clear sight, you can see.

In coming up above you make possible a unitive state.

Emerson said time and space are inverse measures of force of the soul.

Orders that are holy, holy orders, whole, order, ordinary.

In this dimension, it is dim to forget that others dim exist.

Be whole or holy, best all the time not just the one day meant for rest.

We come, come up, communicate, commune up, unite and unify.

A person of intense action with alignment may reach states unsought.

Joy, ecstasy, rapture, bliss, awe, humility, reverence, splendour.

The self-to-true-self explored has freedom to leave the self for others.

Seek the peak through the clouds and rain but for the plateau you should then aim.

Peak states or bliss come to those who have worked on and applied themselves.

If lain or slain, you must have sain, too sane you cannot be, saying.

Sounding like a tuning fork that draws and vibrates harmoniously.

Balance between great opposing forces leaves the freedom to perceive.

Vesica piscis is the space created by the heavens and earth.

Hara, the heart, the head aligned makes balance and peace easy to find.

While working in the world we can still find our nervous system growing.

Sushumna, kundalini, spinal cord, axis to sahasrara.

Some see beings moving from our world to higher, Mercury, Lugh.

At some stage we can awaken, snap out of it, see the spell wear off.

We awoke somewhat but began to doze, thawed some way but then we froze.

Aware of true self, aligned within and without we still climb to wake.

Awakening is when you have felt a level above where you dwelt.

Awakening is where you stand up and realise you have knelt.

Awakening is a way away from a sleepy path mistaken.

Awe of dew at dawn are jewels in the sunlight of the future day.

The first state of transcendence is inside, then outside, then together.

Heavenly Eros flowed through the gate and then grows to meet with agape.

The reach upwards can only flourish when roots are sufficiently deep.

Climb the spire on deep foundations be inspired, point up, point high.

Seven to eight tips the heavenly movement with the magic weight.

At the centre of torus is a channel that allows upwardness.

Mountains strong allow you see far, close to the gates of airy heaven.

Pagoda, minaret, ziggurat, round tower, lighthouse, bell tower.

If pontiff comes from bridge, become it yourself, be your own oracle.

9.2   Drawing the Veil

We must then pierce the veil to get to the holy grail in all the tales.

Tree of life, tree inside us, the roots below, the crown above, all one.

The base must be balanced and great before the person seeks to rise up.

Gape over gap axed, ape to apex grappling, grapes of agape pegged.

To the rose rose light from the garden of the heart and the body core.

The secret of the golden flower, silver moon, open the skylight.

Beauty in the ghost is delivered, given up early, before death.

Immortal emerges in open pavilion on the mountain.

The peacock fans its tail and reveals the glory compressed, awaiting.

Energy reaches bindu point, higher, enthusiasm the point.

Non-ordinary, extraordinary, supreme, milk rise to cream.

At indigo evening we see things in a limited, grander way.

In the evening, the silver moon reflects the light of the sunshine.

On this plane we should train to transcend mundane materiality.

While accepting lower reality we must garner the higher.

Forces can manifest in what is regarded as the sacred.

Letting go and being childlike lets us open to the higher.

After reveille seek the relevant in spirit for revelation.

To function in mundane we must recognise, unify opposites.

The feminine aspect must be balanced to see the whole, feel, connect.

The telestrion is probable chamber of communication.

The sky goddess, sky woman or angel may appear to usher in.

Goddess is fierce in protection but gentle in coaxing, enticing.

Miranda's compassion triumphs then over Prospero's rough magic.

Unify the good with joy in you to create ease, avoid disease.

Reflect on the sacred geometry to help structure consciousness.

Eight, octave, infinity, as above so below, human, om, home.

Darkest hour in the long night of the soul before dawn breaks golden.

Kama, karma, ka, Kali, kami, Kano, kaon, Kamala.

Kabbala, Ka-Ba-Ankh, Kaaba in cosmological unity.

We seek apotheosis, divinization not divination.

"He does not see through the soul nor through the spirit but ..mind...between."

Jacaranda blooms as turtle dove announces promise of presence.

9.3 Healing Way

The true self on its journey with clarity allows itself transform.

Belief based on discipline founded on feeling focuses growth.

Change frequency in your mind and circumvent previous obstacles.

Create a field with your mind and spirit to connect to other fields.

Mythic separation of the sky and the earth kingdoms then repairs.

We must have resistance from self-control and create resonance.

To grow we feel, sense, are intuitive, perceive and empathise.

Only one person has control over the decision to grow.

Master yourself through letting go of negative, seek the fairer land.

Joy and humour rather than pious and po-faced are the path.

Joy, kindness, care, exploration, contemplation, healing are the way.

Consistent with the physical body the spirit body can heal.

Healing is inside, while uniting opposites, flowing energy.

Release the kingfisher or fisher king that has become trapped or hooked.

Perfection is not human, to err is, sainthood is not a prerequisite.

That you tend to anger are foolish, make mistakes is not the end.

Always seek calm, tranquility even when you must face the lion.

The name of the great feminine spirit varies but not its nature.

Sophia flows through those whose feelings allow energy intercede.

Only with expression of the individual heart can seeds spread.

Heka was divine, original, magical, healing energy.

All see creative, powerful, pre-existing energy in us.

9.4 Heart

Warm hearth glowing at an inn on a winter's night is the heart in us.

We must allow a heart of flesh and spirit and not stone or metal.

Love is evolved consciousness, the first four letters of evolution.

Possibilities come from accord between our base and the heavens.

Seek accord within and without, lower and higher, above, below.

Contemplation is the quiet creation of space for the heart.

Anahata the vermillion pavilion lotus in the green site within us.

The heart is the centre of consciousness and not the head on its own.

Sentiment was turned into weakness but heartfelt is truly strong.

Hark, the treasure chests, the ark, the arcanum you seek, are in the heart.

Chest, not but a dead thing made from wood, once living, now housing the good.

Get off your chest that which is heavy on the heart but not with malice.

Why is the heart chakra green? So it can grow and change.

The heart must be like a tortoise able to withdraw from predators.

A, ah, am, awe, awh, awake, who, hu, I, oh, hoo, hum, amen.

A destructive consciousness of the universe must be avoided.

Battle is in human heart and consciousness and not a bloody stage.

The universe is made of vibration you must develop your feel for it.

The heart is the gateway the mind must pass through.

The heart overcomes ego, balances head, reforms relationships.

Transcendence relates to our inner journey and the link is inner.

Transcendent consciousness permeates and is spread throughout the cosmos.

Some call the sutrama the link between the heart and higher will.

There is also the 'heavenly heart' which is the heart of the brain.

We are the stuff that dreams are made on that make dreams inside and out.

What is mine is now a mine of meaning therein, within and without.

Heart has a longing, yearning to come home to its house after roaming.

Temples, tabernacles reflect that there available within you.

Chapel and escape come from word for cape. Be yourself and open up.

Cella or naos was the heart of old temples in ancient worlds.

The deity was often represented in the cella within.

Cell in biology, cella in temple, unit of universe.

9.5 Suscipient

Suscipient, someone who receives, especially a sacrament.

Cosmic consciousness has its receptors in the individual.

The whole is greater, greatest is that, something is that, that is in you.

Reduce cognitive process and conscious thought to reduce resistance.

Ante lucem, before light, antelucan. Antenna getting light.

The word 'kabbalah' revolves around the conception of reception.

Some distinguish the psychics and the pneumatics that may seem same here.

The transcendent consciousness has a mirror in the conscious self.

Mirror needs to be polished and its dish needs to be empty and clear.

Inspiration comes to those who are open and clearly receiving.

Shower of grace falls on those opened up, not sheltering from it.

The bird alights on the still so does spirit descend on the receiver.

The beautiful construct can come unbidden from afar and beyond.

The body may notice slight changes like a soft fuzz around the head.

In then out, insight, invention, intuition, illumination.

I am magnetic, magic, let this go get me to anticipate.

I am in imagination, I am magi, I am game for it.

Created in the image with imaginal to be imago.

The ladder, the golden thread is not in anyone else's control.

Caduceus, golden flower, pearl flowing light, unfolds, uncover.

Transfixed with the transmundane and supernal causes the attraction.

We learn to turn on and off the currents and contexts of consciousness.

We rise up the pillar of light to the celestial parts above.

Our roots and foundation down must be stable to allow the rise up.

Sublime around and soul sounds rhymes and at times when we open towards it.

The sublime is the pull that lulls the push of sublimated ego.

Red and blue combines, purple, amethyst, lavender, violet.

In I oh rainbow and rainbow bridge unite the lain and sky edge.

Sagittarius with firm thigh shoots an arrow into the sky.

The dragon is seen, understood, controlled and marshalled.

Lithe, blithe, bliss, sublime, blessed, blaze, blast, last, latent, exhilaration.

Look up to the stained glass rose windows, contemplate temple templates.

There is beyond sorrow fierce rapture to capture, the arrow to pierce.

Awake aeon, aery, aerial, ariel, aria, arti.

Chapter 10

Nexus to Numinous

10.1 Nexus

Mystic commitment manifests as a mountain path in the mist.

Those who follow the way eventually come to higher ground.

There is a spiral stairs that mystical experience makes known.

There is a sun door that opens a light box in the mound of matter.

Pushing to true self and transcending, punctures to let in overtures.

When we align we allow the loving intelligence manifest.

With what do we aim to accord? All rivers will run to the same sea.

The canals or lakes on the way that are dammed are like it, but not it.

We come to the threshold through a path after a long road reflecting.

We ascend the spiral as the self has lightened and the path is sure.

Into the vestibule of the rosy zone, one's own, beyond known.

It is the reaching of the source in the old Zen story of Ten Bulls.

It is the pouring in of spirit from above that matches within.

It is the cataclysmic rod receiving the deluge washing down.

Pure consciousness revisited burns the paper walls of illusion.

Instead of thinking about a destination think journey, process.

Interpretations of the mystical end are not then critical.

Processes and practices and preparation produce potential.

Call the link of intention, superconsciousness, beyond- the 'nexus.'

The nexus lets flow upwards and downwards, inwards and outwards to us.

For some they want to be emptied and for some they want to be filled.

It also could be called the zenith, or the zenith nexus instead.

It could be called lumen which means light and cavity in a body tube.

It could be centre of mystical accord, harmonious union with universe.

"Wholly on heavenly things my mind is set..., so streams do show the head."

It is as spirit proboscis like on our head to feed from forward.

On the calvarium, in place of skulls, sutures cross at fontanelle.

It is superior scala from the scintilla of divine spark.

Context of mysticism has changed and reframing is extension.

Convergent sequence, centripetal-centrifugal, zenith-nadir.

It could be the re-uniting of our shen below with shen around.

We conduce, conduct, make condyle, bring it together through conduit.

That it is, is more important than what it is, that always recurs.

The cultivation of the higher link is at the basis of all.

It's middle pillar on firm foundation in operation for some.

As a Star Trek teleportation device for the soul to transport.

Dadirri for Aboriginals is inner spring of the divine.

"...Pentecost was fully come they were all with one accord in one place."

Churches often had Holy Ghost holes in the dome to let spirit in.

Proliferation of new powers is not its object or its end.

But many uncover possibilities, paranormalities.

Ecsomatic, flow within the body, beyond analysis.

The cloud of unknowing is pierced by the arrow of the heart's focus.

It is the sent beam of ghostly light piercing this cloud of unknowing.

It is Saraha's arrow got from the arrow-making Dakini.

It is Emerson's said openness to influx of light and power.

It is the path to the covenant with the universal wisdom.

Like cilia on cell ceiling feeling for el cielo sealing low.

Spiritual practice acts to elevate us to the highest.

It is sought sense of fusion with the Absolute and retreat as well.

We retreat to the mortal and mundane to live one world at a time.

The enrichment, nourishment of spiritual mind imbues our life.

Oneness is the force we re-connect our power with or we wither.

To some it is advaita or non-duality, oneness obtained.

All then can initiate into our initial, inner being.

Mystical unity instantiates universal essence.

In all alone fountainhead can flow, as tall everyone's thoughts can go.

For some it is energy, light into that we see as our matter.

An aperture to the apercu, a priori, a prior eye.

Pantheon has an oculus with gods underneath higher opening.

Invisible middle pillar rises up to sky from earth through you.

The shaman climbs the pole to communicate with the gods in the sky.

Pole, wand, sceptre, mace, sword, obelisk, staff, crook, flail symbol of nexus?

Djed in Egypt symbolised the link through the body to higher life.

Like Birkeland currents, like Tesla's coil, understanding of old remains.

Individual in right breathing can connect to the universe.

Crown, corona, aura, aurora, aureola, august, auspice.

Circulation of light within through our inner energy occurs.

We seek a communion not the communal, an ascent not descent.

To some soul unites with or marries the spirit or higher angels.

To some it is an aligning of centres of body energy.

Capricorn, strong-legged unicorn, unseen legend connected.

Really ally earthily and ethereally in real relay.

Infusione, internuncio, interfluent, influence.

Interoperability here inlaid in aid of therapy.

Uraeus in Egypt was a symbol of the nexus rising up.

Henosis was the Greek word for union, column of spirit.

True yoga is union, Atman-Brahman, true, absolute self and cosmos.

Tantric union is the way duality balanced to connect some.

Sophia perennis emerges out like bioluminescence.

Red crown of Egypt has a proboscis on top, the link to heaven.

Buddha's ushnisha symbolised spiritual link to universe.

The peak state comes to those who have actualised and worked clearly.

Now is the winter of discontent made glorious summer by work.

Peak states may punctuate normality, if more can become plateau.

Up the tree we reach the treasure, insight the key, vision the pleasure.

We really climb up a branch that leads to the trunk and heavenly roots.

Nexus comes from the Latin word to bind. It means connection or link.

Nexus is an harmonious union and an accord, chord or cord.

The nexus of deep meaning like gold, dusty sky at evening.

Nexus could be axis mundi of us under, up to heavens.

To some it is the antahkarana, a bridge or column of light.

To some it is theosis, after theoria and catharsis.

Time and space is elastic, transcendent in certain circumstances.

The heart of The Magic Flute is Mozart's art of spirit and nexus.

Ravished, rapture, rapt is a union not the rupture of the raptors.

The secret stairs to reach the stars, focus on its fare bliss deep up it.

From the earth up through cleared channels to the celestial is the link.

Like on a space elevator, we seek the heights to gain perspective.

Nexus is not monopoly of any leader or religion.

For you who have worked hard at it, euphoria you have created.

As below will only bring as above mirrored and magnified.

This is the zone of white light that induces vivid calm in vision.

The link comes from earth and meets with the heavens, the silver cord connects.

The soul seeks ascension through the ones that are the way, the truth and life.

The force which pushes towards correct paths then pulls to source in balance.

Lose time, space, inhibition, fear, doubt, self-criticism sensation.

Feel as one, free, expressive, realised and spontaneous being.

Influence means to flow in. Influence and then influence without.

Influx with flux within or without is flowing like water in flume.

Next influx, nexus fit unto us, fusion to use to fix fissures.

You are never alone but you can be cut off without connection.

The nexus is a link to your higher self and higher consciousness.

The spirit has an umbilical cord to higher consciousness.

Choice of nexus is open to most, align and begin to ascend.

Nexus is a link to the numinous open to varying degrees.

Nexus may be woven slowly with sense of inevitability.

Nexus may come instead as a dam bursting but after alignment.

Nexus may be likened to a tree, cord, cloud, hill, channel or tunnel.

Nectar of the heavens comes through nexus, yin above and yang below.

Nexus is the path to union many mystics and others describe.

It might be the symbol of horn of the unicorn, union in it.

Mystic union is immit, immerging, immersion, immingling.

Union is me of the mortal re-meeting the more immortal.

Ineffable, not fabled, enabling some who pursue all the way through.

Immixed or imbuing with the immense and the immemorial.

The experience is the same type whatever the name of the game.

It is ultimate force of what they conceive whatever the name.

Oneness, unity, pure consciousness or Absolute apprehension.

The transmutation or shape shifting or the Absolute absorption.

What it is depends but has to be the highest possibility.

Intimidating intimate not to describe but intimate.

Out of top of cupola of the Duomo, view the panorama.

Above and below may oscillate movement like light through the stargate.

Intelligence within resonates with intelligence without.

Being like reception, intussusception of consciousness in us.

In the creation of nexus the inner and the outer merge.

The compassionate creative heart is a magnet for the nexus.

Creativity and compassion are critical paths in the nexus.

Great carers and creatives have been open to the gifts of the air.

10.2 Numinous

Numinous is spirit arousing, awe-inspiring, luminous.

Numinous is the opening up of the infinite channel.

Numinous is then towards the nirvanic, kevala jnana for some.

Numinous towards the non-duality, the utmost. Superessence.

Where we aspire is the spire top of us in the sky up there.

We finally become aware of our final awareness to seek.

Like the stork we build the nest of ourself on a high panorama.

Nothing may become everything and everything may become empty.

It is the mystery in the mystery itself beyond concepts.

It is realm of apocalypse beyond the calypso of life.

It is intention focused in ideal form synchronised, put up there.

Experience takes precedence over opinion of an 'expert.'

Experts may have no experience of their subject of expertise.

Experiments cannot expect to explain all experience.

The experience of the highest things are beyond experience.

The fondest, great treasures are beyond measure, beware the measurers.

To some there, non-duality, illumination, buddhanature.

God is a human word wielding more power than yielding meaning.

They seek to make it ordinary and not leave The Unbeknownst.

That which is utter is unutterable and should not be uttered.

The force behind meaning remains if reason and ridicule obscure.

Love is the force of the universe that forms food for the spirit.

If God has been obscured for you think supermeaning, ideal archetype.

Some call it non-local consciousness like a pool there to swim in.

That thing cannot be just anything you make it or want it to be.

That can never be something that we can construct, design or manage.

God is never solely human and we should never seek to be God.

It could be the Infinite Awareness, VALIS, the Arche, the Not.

Think Absolute Being, Ultimate Reality, Supreme Being.

Infinite Spirit, The One or even the greatest consciousness.

Nirvana, oneness, eternity, satori, samyama, heavens.

Nirvana means blown out, a type of exsufflation, extinguishing.

The unio mystica comes from the nexus for some, or is it.

Mystical union is a source of insight and knowledge to mystics.

It could be devekut to some, clinging or cleaving to the divine.

For many it is that which is not, never just that which appears.

Providence provided being, being that that can be seen from now.

Reflection of the pleroma, plural, pointed, plentifulness.

A sense of immortality, illumination, loss of death fear.

Does anyone control divine, own it, know it better than itself?

The awe and mystery cannot be explained but only suggested.

Indescribable, so only indicia to experience.

Human, numen, new men, new women, noumenon, nod to the divine.

Every person is gifted with potential of great aliveness.

Theophanic is the counterpoint to the panic of pointlessness.

Immanence is permeation of universe with intelligence.

Diamond sparkle of the dazzling night dwells within in your own light.

Things you have seen are more vital like green now yellowy, gold and blue.

After connection more paths open and blind alleys close.

Invention means to 'come in,' initiating higher imprints.

All souls are magnets that are evolved to attract repel or be still.

Majestic, magenta, magnificent, magnum opus and matrix.

Magenta agent of age of magis imagining images.

Trickster may be a manifestation of pathfinder to nexus.

Integrated consciousness within allows the integration without.

Linking to higher consciousness will make in and out less relevant.

We open to allow inflow, insight, inspiration, instinct.

To heal, be holy, be whole, be holistic and integrate wholly.

Imagination is bridge between inner and outer consciousness.

Beethoven's Ninth Symphony, Van Gogh Sunflowers reflect the link.

Plato and Pythagoras learned and showed the inherent here from there.

Satchitananda, you exist, you are bliss, thou art that, you are light.

Some would so seek Buddha or Christ consciousness some others Osiris.

Some see connection to angels, guardian angels or fravarti.

In certain circumstances we can perceive the past and the future.

Droplets form, the raintree falling silent makes ripples on silver pools.

Death is not to be feared by the enlightened. Best effort, no regrets.

Battle is between those who want to cut the cord and those who do not.

Grace is gifted not grafted to allow the ether of clarity.

The spring rises, evaporates in sunshine, condensation falls.

In the vortex of energy, the spirit can move more freely.

Upper and lower link across a chasm of doubt and delusion.

There is a clear and integral healing insight that comes through with ease.

Druid signals there is a sacred dove, portal means awakening.

Sun shines into the chamber of stones on mound so does nexus occur.

Home, the promised land of milk and honey, the unified kingdom come.

May heavens secrete secrets to those who seek the way to integrate.

The yang, the male is balanced with the brown earth, Sophia ascendant.

Yin above, yang below, both gyres intersect and alternate.

The nexus may be Atman to Brahman, Te and Tao, Jacob's Ladder.

Great Spirit, Holy Spirit, Brahman, God, One, Ishvara the unknown name?

You do not need to believe, to recite, to know to experience.

It is an Indra's net of computer hardware with ether software.

It is the concept of the chariot and merkaba in the link.

Yonder lies the place beyond time and space, not local not confined.

Immerse yourself in the imminent immanent to seek immanence.

Make your consciousness resident of this state or present there at will.

To sip from nectar alone without applying gifts is entropy.

Realisation cannot remain unmanifested in mundane.

We look and learn from the stars with our feet on the ground then we reach.

Linking to the numinous means creation of the absolute self.

The absolute self is the tinder and kindling for divine spark.

Aquarius, bindu, da'at, heaven knows, vessel fills, overflows.

Pisces is illumination, coming after the long, dark struggle.

Ineffability, beauty and peace beyond words beckon beyond.

Levels of spiritual bliss can get higher to the ultimate.

It is sahaja samadhi, working in reality, aware.

Realisation of the interconnectedness of spirit occurs.

Glimpsing beyond, the ultimate changes even if that happens once.

Some say familiarity with numinous creates projection.

Above water the great crested grebe moves, below just as elegant.

Hopkins had hope but he foundered below heavenly horizons.

Numinous is not the domain we remain in yet but integrate.

You alone are confectionary, confederacy of being.

But reaching the source we must return refreshed to society.

We strive then to arrive because belonging is the deepest longing.

Spiritual seekers seek that sought because it ought to be wrought.

Seek elevation in consciousness because we are meant to grow so.

There are higher levels of spiritual perception, mystic knows.

Finding fuller consciousness is like an Amazon that flows through you.

That mystics take a world within does not the external world remake.

Mystics getting insights does not make many outsights less troubling.

Mystics dark places go or have been, terrible things can't be unseen.

Mystical mindsets may not pay bills so we focus on outside still.

Still emerges the found heavenly around and in us to submerge.

Chapter 11

Mechanics

11.1 Threats to Spirit

My granny I thought mad, the Muppets - 'They're taking over the world.'

Technology will divide those who will be machine slaves and not.

Technology will imprint the labyrinth technocracy wishes.

We being spirit owned and possessed forever as we allow it.

Machine has a chime of ache in it inching its way to break us down.

Way of the prophet is far less compelling than that of profit.

When told you never had it so good look for what is lost forever.

When the world is truly split the splitters will blame non-science on it.

Conquered peoples are curiously captured with trifles, trinkets.

Commerce and power will aways seek to control the profitable.

Control will hem in the human reduced through their own servility.

Centrifugal force of western civil war reason will endorse.

Capacity to assimilate machines is incommensurate.

Many who study consciousness do so to facilitate control.

Spiritual reality of interconnectedness hijacked.

Science will sacrifice some prejudices to capture our consciousness.

If to science, spirit, consciousness we leave, destiny will grieve.

Many think we have but a blind dogma of the ghost in the machine.

They think that the machine is all and the ghost a fantastic fable.

Then they say that we should worship the machine and yield gladly to it.

Machines will never get deepest human thinking but humans lose it.

First they will deny and dismiss the precious things you already possess.

Then they invert and appropriate terms and concepts that can be used.

They will try to measure, reduce and locate that which can be controlled.

The machines and technology will be presented as salvation.

Freedom is always a state of mind and not the mind of the state.

By their fruits will you know them, see what words and techniques aspire to.

Observe freedom's obsequies obsequiousness to oblivion.

Obloquy to those who seek to block what they see will be obsessive.

Free will will be denied and derided and then freedom will have died.

You'll be told that your consciousness is merely about information.

You will be called a machine of meat whose salvation is more machines.

Every reduction of human spirit ends up a circular saw.

Science will beg the question and accuse others of doing the same.

Beware collectivisation of individual consciousness.

End of black magic may be tragic trend of technology control.

Mayhap mayhem may mar them dreams we may it seem ourselves then entrap.

Inauthentic prophets of consciousness seek to rob your divine gift.

They deny soul's survival, but want to download mind to computer.

They never tire telling the dire need to retire fire.

Mechanical mindsets magnify the might of new technology.

Transhumanism is humans in trance to be machine enslaved.

Transhumanism allows monopolisation of transcendent.

Technology we use as instruments will soon use us fools as tools.

Pancosmism, pandemic, pandemonium, Pandora's box.

The higher is gained by ignoring ours in favour of machines.

'Singularity' desired is sired with sigil, sin in it.

Absent an effort to wake up we remain robots and machines.

Those escaping the wired, wireless or wi-fi will be weird.

Some see Ahriman as a manifestation of machine spirit.

The final ordeal of humanity is dealing with the machine, threats and benefits.

You who have spirit and are cautious of machines will be the liars.

Dynamo go, so cello and cella to dying in a prison cell.

War machines independently demand and expect sacrifices.

Great magic is really science and great science is really magic.

Achievements of science and technology are awesome, pervasive.

Biggest threat comes from the smallest it isolates, discovers, creates.

The fascination with the artificial may invite disaster.

Mechanical mindsets may make a world familiar to them.

Machines are tools but it seems a new priesthood wants to install themselves.

Machines will get the power of attention when humans have lost it.

Many interested in consciousness want to rob it for machines.

Many are those who will destroy complexity to tinker with trifles.

Many Star Chambers may manifest in a network of oppression.

Every time has its own unique effect on the mind and body.

Evolution of spirit must always counteract some great danger.

Abnegation of life and spirit is a perennial danger.

There is an ongoing war against beings that want to be free.

Freedom could be crushed into a marginal zone of fake virtue.

Destructive forces from history have not disappeared but alter.

Destructive forces fight, alter but their altar seeks sacrifices.

The unfeeling find it easy to dominate distracted feeling.

Spirit must not be alienated by the mechanistic.

Spirit is valuable and the mechanical is not spiritual.

A web can easily extend the control of a predator.

The net is a borrowed, higher order spiritual concept.

Artificial Intelligence is neither the former nor latter.

AI involves final relinquishing of human autonomy.

Physical time and space can be controlled by malign and malignant.

The mechanical cloud is an inversion of spiritual cloud.

People unknowing are becoming lab rats in an experiment.

We are now cyborgs by design leaving spirit to forces malign.

11.2 Technos

Technology enchants the brain while disenchanting spirit and world.

Technology may increase doing at the expense of being.

Put aside for a moment the great good technology may us bring.

Technology can also bind us with the power of The One Ring.

As well as uses we are finding technology is spellbinding.

Technology is product of both science and creative spirit.

Without mystical scientists and events, science would be much less.

Science through scientism attacking the spirit is monstruous.

Science will allow itself be worshipped as an ends and not means.

Technology is instrument of control of commercial science.

Technology is like the risen sun of the new god of science.

Technology will be used to take the spiritus away from us.

Let us call worship of technology the religion of 'technos.'

Technology is an effective weapon for mass mesmerism.

Post to posterity resignation from responsibility.

The hypnotised can be turned into zombies by technology.

Technology may be an instrument of hubris and ignorance.

The story of suppression of spirit by mechanical unfolds.

Atheism is sometimes a part of an attempt to control the psyche.

Technos is the worship of the god of control and subjugation.

We are writing a suicide note for humanity in code.

They shatter panes between good and bad prodding with a million splinters.

No good nor bad just dynamic dogma that is correct or computes.

New material gods with devised morals substitute the divine.

Desire for machine mesmerism makes some sire our demise.

Discontent with our world we make a quagmire of the abode.

Abiding hid, amid a bad, mad din of ideas made machine.

Narcissism is psychological noose allowing entrapment.

Heart-haters help create machines that threaten spirit reality.

The imprisonment of psyche is part of armageddon.

Technology is an instrument of the mistaken desire to be godlike.

True technology exists to meet the needs of free humanity.

Daedalus worked with The Man, making us Narcissus and Tantalus.

The coming age can be one of mercenaries, castles, vassals, serfs.

Priesthoods always interpose themselves between spirit and beyond.

Technocracy, mock aristocracy arising to take us in.

Recreating nature is an enemy, don't abandon garden.

Biggest control from smallest, weakness furnishes opposing strength.

Combination, sorcery, power lust create enemies of good.

Dark harvests already sown must be reaped before lessons are learned.

Spirals of spirits evolve and pass over previous selves.

Biggest threat to humanity will come through form of the smallest things.

The strongest opponent to humans will arise from its weakest traits.

Mysticism is co-opted through group as God-denying tool.

Many will be the mystics who falsely lead and confuse. Learn your way.

The sacred birch can lead to Birkeland currents, wigwam or Birkenau.

Poetry, parable, metaphor, soft things that trouble machine mind.

Hawking was right about the threat of AI to human existence.

AI, DMT, evolutionary psychology isn't God.

Code that we allowed to become king is slavery in the making.

Newton knew many things but we then forget to know his mystic life.

Blake thought that Art was the Tree of Life. Science was the Tree of Death.

Blake knew that philosophers did not know the causes of things found.

Blake wrote that Reason is not the same it shall be when we know More.

Blake wrote that 'All you behold tho' it appears Without it is Within.'

Blake thought Reason was a state but imagination was existence.

All things exist in imagination and in our experience.

Chapter 12

The Star: The Hope

12.1 Elaboration

The true language of the spiritual consciousness is love.

Pure water gives life, poisoned it makes wilt. Do not wilt as thou will do.

Riddle this sceptic, what if the spiritual universe is true?

Forget the con artist, tricksters, desperate and deluded in it.

Ignore the nutritionless, institutional farming of spirit.

Avoid the senseless septic set of sects and sectarianism.

Let science do some good things but oppose its religionisation.

Science requires belief too. Do you believe in the Big Bang then?

Science and reason balanced one issue and then became the problem.

Learn from science, leave scientism, recover enlightenment.

Be disciplined in mind, critical, open and compassionate.

You might be weird, but that meant ability to control destiny.

Hope is of balance between benign materialism and our inherent nature.

Break the surly bonds, sirly binds, sourly bounds, sorry bands.

Self clears, knowing well with attention, transcending to link numinous.

A mystical accord seeks to be a sound in harmony with life.

Model, mode of the mystics is an ode to seeking, solving suddenly.

Mysticism is an antidote to forces of the ant, machines.

Many may not yet know mystic reality but model informs.

It might be the infinite way to some or the Tao to some others.

Good activity comes to those whose toes are in mud reaching for stars.

Some wanted to be angels, but we find our better angels within.

The temple is in us beyond all reach of others, untouchable.

Feel gratitude, grace, gifted the best, attitude, embrace, shift blest.

Higher levels of consciousness open spirit growing heavenly.

Your powers grow and reveal although they are not the main objective.

The nexus allows us to go through the pass to the great potential.

Joyful attitude is a buoy in strife and vicissitudes of life.

There are some who wish to escape, enlightened and drift away in clouds.

Most who raise their unique self up learn to adapt like crocodiles.

Metaphysics merely a box that can't capture feeling sincerely.

High peace brings a loss of doubt about who and what you are or can be.

But the dove can move swiftly to avoid the eagle. Vigilance and awareness.

The end of the journey for some is moksha, mukti or nirvana.

Old abilities can be invoked to deal with newer challenges.

Many ways are there but certain gates are few and only there for you.

Purpose may be modest or great but if true to you, you gladly do.

Seer steer to mightier pier to pierce and peer at tier beyond fear.

Make mandalas for mind to focus on the pattern of progression.

We are inventions, come in that we can re-invent ourselves.

Construct your own sigils to signify and signal your seity.

Endeavour of exploration will evoke and gain peace more than pain.

Move with the wave you wait for and not against it, to carry to shore.

Angels await those hearts that yearn for eternally positive.

Calm, relaxed you ought to be ready for any the onslaught to see.

Feel, desire, wish, ask, attract, intend, focus, realise, invent.

Cycle of curiosity, creativity, compassion, care.

Aboriginals have something you shouldn't under-estimate.

Learn about systems, how they work and what implications they have.

All systems require roles, flows, inputs, outputs, causes and effects.

Meaning in meandering, application is unforeseeable.

Numbers, shapes, patterns, signs, symbols, sigils, signals help us clarify.

Whether philosophy works can be seen on long trajectory.

Distill your words, bestill your doubts and get your message to others.

The essential mission is to engage in your spiritual growth.

The whole person seeks to come in accord with the waves of existence.

Fear not unfathomable future and fear fear by ignoring it.

Be aware of yin, yang, flow, force, paradox, simple observation.

The time then comes to come out and show your face and sow your seed.

Fences, fake false few resources that can easily be broken down.

Better be boldly alone than one of the sheep in the pen.

The energy to persist is there and the path is clear, keep on it.

You know the clues make sense, to separate the process from the pretence.

Powers within are phenomenal that is what we must believe.

You must know it, express it and get your message not ex libris.

Crossing the rubicon of doubt makes it clear about reaching the goal.

You don't have courage and build it up over a chasm of doubt.

Massage, manipulation of the body helps the spirit to flow.

Massage with consciousness of consciousness is a forgotten path.

Simplicity with meaningfulness, clarity with complexity.

Things you may be embarrassed about you transmute to become proud of.

Who has what you want? Make it no person by developing yourself.

Rules may be broken if they don't jeopardise the bright prize you seek.

Be capable, a cappella, capital, chapter of your heart.

12.2 Coda

Consciousness is the higher love, love higher the is consciousness.

Mastering your lower self means your higher self can ride the donkey.

Be glad that you have made mistakes for that means that you are human.

You were part of the whole, we depart, grow and return to the fold.

Create momentum, get going, make it, so it makes it then happen.

You can achieve what you believe with mind and heart if you leave doubt out.

There will be light, there will be joy, though you must really trust in yourself.

Your greatest burden may be what gives you lessons if you reflect.

The reality of time is never erased but transmutable.

Now walk tall and be your true, intuitive self, supported, strong.

Seek not retreat, you must eat, beat, feel heat, find your feet, meet, greet, defeat.

Laud not the lotus-eaters or laudanum drinkers but clarity.

Let future transpire, be inspired instead of perspiring.

Your life is a journey whose success is not judged by other people.

Worries are vapours that will vanish like our short time on this planet.

Cherry blossoms spring pink as tree grows, heals and takes from up and down.

The right spiritual path does not preclude use of assertive means.

Dwell on rose and lotus, pink lotus, golden gate, silver gate and key.

Out with doubt about your bigger powers, do not look back but forward.

The choice to respond with strength and humour is always ours finally.

Spirit like a lit candle, be light not dark, light not heavy, watermark.

Wheel of will carries chariot of conviction to destination.

Know yourself so you have no doubt and are tranquil, at peace and clear.

Every person has possibility, gift of seeking accord.

The mystical accord is as perennial as the grass growing.

The mystical accord describes and suggests it, but is not all it.

The mystical accord is the chord of the cord of the universe.

Invest the best of yourself in your growth, integration and sharing.

Your spirit must ascend, evolve, ascend and tend to other persons.

Great, guest sages of the ages, guess, gauge, gauze, assuage the year's gears.

Aegis against technological magic is mystical accord.

Amphibiously we live in the amphitheatre and the gods.

Accordingly, accord, a cord, at one, atone, a tone, at once.

Ascension beyond duality to being one, like one, returned.

True self, spirit centre, aware of itself is elementary.

Most mystic roses were born to blush unseen, we don't know they have been.

If you have found your diamond within, it can be brought around, beyond.

Time to relinquish all to esoteric, religious structures ends.

Mystic accord, way, vocation, path, open up, feel it and fear not.

Allow not self a worrycow be through living fear only you see.

Spirit sum is much more than the symposium of all your thoughts.

Spirit is silkie on land seeking and knowing the sea is sought.

So self cures itself to be drawn to mystic places where it ought to.

Mystic in you there for a reason, never going out of season.

There is in us already a vent, to keep us right it was meant.

Core of Mystical Accord came mainly to me as if from the core.

Partake in the process to remake your world and find your peace within.

All mystical traditions in good faith without ill will can teach us.

If your mystical accord cannot tell right from wrong it is false.

If your mystical accord demands force to impose it is not it.

If your mystical accord is without conscience it is something else.

Care more for a mystical cave and core than the code that will enslave.

To love and to care clear and true are the things we must dare to do.

Setanta, Cuchulainn, Siddharta, Kukulkan, open your eyes.

You must be a spiritual warrior or agent, or a slave.

History is unfolding of war of spirit and material.

Any way can lead to the Way if it is a heart way done right.

Backwards can be forwards if you intend to go to the right end.

Whether you're here or there is neither here nor there if you're aware.

There are those who will cherish spirit and those who will wish it perish.

Eldorado dreams hide Midas shadows you had ever inside.

The mystical accord oddly is also the cataclysmic rod.

No battle is greater than the war for possession of the spirit.

GLOSSARY

A Ah Sha Sa Ma Ha Ancient Buddhist mantra.

Abba (Aramaic) Father.

Aboriginal From Latin 'ab origine' meaning from the beginning.

Absorption The incorporation and often associated transformation.

A capella Unaccompanied song, origin referring to the Italian for 'in the church.'

Acme The highest point, culmination.

Acupressure Pressure applied to acupoints.

Adam The first man, first human or humans.

Adamah (Hebrew) Ground or earth.

Adumbrate To outline or indicate the shadow.

Advaita (Sanskrit) Vedantic doctrine of non-duality.

Aegis A protective shield in Greek mythology.

Aeon Very long time or a power from the supreme deity.

Aery Spiritual, aerial.

Agape A word of Greek origin to describe a type of transcendent or highest love, significant in Christian theology.

Aghora (Sanskrit) Group who seek non-duality through embracing social taboos.

Ah A mantra believed to be sacred by some.

Ahimsa (Sanskrit) Principle of not harming beings.

Ahriman The dark spirit in Zorastrianism.

AI Artificial intelligence.

Alchemy The art of transmutation.

Alexander, Eben Author of *Proof of Heaven: A Neurosurgeon's Journey into the Afterlife*.

Alkahest Supposed solvent of the alchemists.

Amen End of prayer, concluding, assent, true.

Amun-Ra Egyptian god of great significance.

Anahata (Sanskrit) Heart chakra.

Anam (Irish) Soul.

Anamnesis Going back to Socrates and Plato, an idea of knowledge that is innate or inspired.

'And it is not possible for a servant to serve two masters.' *Gospel of St. Thomas.*

'And wheresoever thou mayest be, thou art a stranger and pilgrim' From *Of The Imitation of Christ.* Thomas A Kempis. 1470.

Antahkarana (Sanskrit) Inner cause, generally seen as a linking force or channel between separable elements of the being.

Ante lucem (Latin) Before light, antelucan.

Apercu Immediate, intuitive insight.

Apocalypse While often understood as a great conflagration or showdown between good and evil, it more consistently refers to a great revelation whereby some great spiritual truth is uncovered in a vision often about the end times.

Apophenia Tendency to seek patterns in random information.

Apotheosis Deification.

Apperceive To perceive, conscious of perceiving.

A priori Reasoning from what is prior.

Arcana (Singular) **Arcanum** Secret or mystery.

Archangel Highest of the angels, e.g Michael, Gabriel, Raphael.

Arche Something that was in the beginning, a primal element.

Archetype Original pattern or model.

Archon Beings recognised by the Gnostics.

Arco (Italian) Bow.

Argot Jargon of a particular group.

Aria Melody or air often with vocal solo.

Ariel A spirit of the air. A character in *The Tempest.*

Aries   Ram. First sign of zodiac.

Aristotle (384-322 BC)   Great philosopher and scientist.

Armageddon   Scene of the battlefield between good and evil, from the Book of Revelation in the New Testament.

Arti (Sanskrit)   Hindu religious practice involving lighted wicks in oil.

As above, so below   An hermetic principle.

Asah Shamah (Hebrew)   By doing, we understand-Israelite response to obtaining the Book of the Covenant.

Asomatic   Being unaware of being associated with a body or entity.

Assoil   Expiate, clear.

Assuage   To soften.

Atman (Sanskrit)   Inner self or soul.

Aton   Sun disc with rays or sun god in Ancient Egypt.

Aura   From the Latin for breath, used to refer to human energy field.

Aureola   Glorifying halo.

Auspice   Omen drawn from looking at birds.

Automaton   Self operating machine or a person who operates in a mechanical or unemotional way.

Avatar   Deity manifested in human form.

Avidya (Sanskrit)   Ignorance

Axis Mundi   A point regarded as the centre of the world, often used as a connection between heaven and earth.

Ayahuasca   A plant that is used in a concoction that allows DMT affect the brain.

Ayurveda (Sanskrit)   Indian system of medicine.

Azan   Muslim call to prayer.

Ba   Part of the Egyptian concept of soul.

Baba   Often used for a spiritual leader.

Bandit   Outlaw, robber, someone who takes advantage of.

Baphomet   Idols that the Templars and other were accused of having worshipped.

Bapu (Hindi)   Spiritual father.

Baraka   In certain religions or mystical traditions this is a spiritual, divine force that resides in certain people, places and things.

Barco (Spanish)   Ship or boat.

Barque   Egyptian boat.

BDSM   Bondage and Discipline, Submission and Dominance.

Beauty-in-the-ghost   A phrase used by Gerard Manley Hopkins in the Leaden Echo and the Golden Echo poem.

Beethoven, Ludwig van (1770-1827)   His 9th Symphony is often considered his finest and he, like Mozart was influenced by Indian and Egyptian thought.

Berimbau   One stringed instrument of African origin central to the game of capoeira.

Bindu (Sanskrit)   In Tantra, a point at back of head.

Bioluminescence   Emission of light by a living organism.

Birkeland, Kristian (1867-1917)   Scientist who expounded theories of atmospheric, electric currents.

Birkenau   Death camp part of Auschwitz-Birkenau complex, named after the birch trees that were there.

Black, Jonathan   Author of *The Secret History of the World*.

Black magic   Magic with use of evil spirits or for sinister purposes.

Black maria   Prisoner transport or vehicle.

Blake, William (1757-1827)   Poet, artist, mystic.

Blithe   Joyous.

Boehme, Jacob (1575-1624)   German Christian mystic (also written as Behmen).

Boon   Gift or blessing.

Brahma   First god of the Hindu triad.

Brahman   Eternal absolute impersonal principle.

Caduceus   Actual or symbolic winged wand with two snakes, rod of the messenger of the gods.

Calvarium The uppercase of the brain, the skull cap. The sutures cross where the soft spot was. Calvary and Golgotha were the hill and the place of crucifixion of Jesus. Golgotha is the place of skulls.

Calypso As well as a dance, it refers to the nymph in Greek mythology.

Campbell, Joseph (1904-1987) Professor of literature and author of *The Hero With a Thousand Faces*.

Capoeirista A person who participates in the Afro-Brazilian martial art or game of capoeira. The game may preserve elements of what was an African mystical tradition in it.

Capricorn The Goat, tenth sign of zodiac.

Cataclysmic Comes from the Greek to wash down, deluge or flood.

Cataleptic State of body rigidity.

Cataphysical Unnatural.

Catechism Exposition of doctrine.

Cathar A member of the movement of Christians centres in Southern France with unique views that led to persecution by the Catholic Church.

Catharsis From the Greek word 'katharsis.'

Catheter A thin tube often used medically.

Cathexis A charge of mental energy attached to an object or idea.

Cayce, Edgar (1877-1945) Clairvoyant, healer associated with the New Age by some.

Cella The most sacred part of a temple.

Centrifugal Force directed away from axis of rotation.

Centripetal Force drawing towards a point or a centre.

Chakra The centres of spiritual power in the body, from Sanskrit word for wheel.

Chan Chinese Buddhism.

Charis One of the three graces, the three charities, the Greek goddesses. Origin of the word charisma.

Charon The mythic ferryman in Greek myth who rowed the spirits of the dead across the Styx.

Chi Energy, life force.

Chi Kung Chinese systems of exercises for physical, mental and spiritual health, also qijong.

Chimerical Imaginary, from the chimera, the monstrous hybrid of Greek myth.

Chrysalis From the Greek word for gold, meaning the pupa case.

Cielo, El (Spanish) Heaven, Sky.

Cilia (plural of cilium) Protuberances from the cell body.

Cinnabar Mineral, sulphide of mercury, also called vermillion as a pigment.

Circulatio (Latin) Term meaning revolution or circulation, used in music and often having symbolic meaning.

Clockwork Orange A book by Anthony Burgess in 1962 supposedly based on the saying 'Queer as a clockwork orange' (where 'queer' means strange). It was released as a film in 1971.

Cloud of Unknowing, The The mystical Christian classic from late 1300's originally *The Cloud of Unknowyng*.

Coda Rounding out passage from the Italian word for tail.

Compassion Originally meaning to suffer with, usage usually implies a sympathy, sensitivity and identity with other's suffering and needs.

Concomitant Thing which naturally follows on with something else.

Concord Harmony, agreement, of the same heart. This has been used to describe some of the approaches of Ficino and Pico della Mirandola also. Apart from that, Concord is the town in Massachusetts USA, where Ralph Waldo Emerson, Henry David Thoreau and other Transcendentalists lived.

Condyle Bone for articulation with another.

Confectionary A place where confections are made. A confection is made by combining ingredients.

Confederacy League or alliance.

Contemplatio (Latin) Contemplate.

Convent A place for coming together, usually of nuns.

Conventicle   Secret meeting for religious purposes.

Convention   A large meeting or a norm or practice.

Convergence   Coming together, meeting at a point.

Corona   Crown or halo.

Correspondence   The doctrine or principle of correspondence is a hermetic principle.

Coruscating   Brilliant, sparkling.

Cosmopolitan   Basically a citizen of the world with wide ranging perspectives or relating to the world and diverse sources.

Couer (French)   Heart.

Course in Miracles, A   A book on spiritual transformation by Helen Schucman.

Coven   A gathering of witches.

Crook   Staff of a shepherd or religious leader bent at top.

Crowley, Aleister (1875-1947)   Magician, poet, painter, novelist and mountaineer. Founder of Thelema.

Cuchulainn   In Irish Cú Chulainn, a mythic warrior, formerly Setanta.

Cupola   Vault, ceiling or lantern on top of a dome. In the Duomo in Florence one has a beautiful view of the city and surroundings.

Cure   Healing or preserving.

Curt   Short, concise.

Da'at (Hebrew)   Knowing, secret. The state where the sephira are united.

Daedalus   Greek inventor of labyrinth, father of Icarus, creator of Cretan labyrinth, skilled but myth suggests need to be cautious.

Daemon   A guiding spirit.

Dakini (Tibetan)   Female spiritual being or teacher.

Dandelion   Weed from the French 'dent de lion' (lion's tooth), traditionally used for liver health.

Dante (1265-1351)   The Italian poet Dante Aligheiri who wrote Commedia known as '*The Divine Comedy.*'

Dayadhvam (Sanskrit)   Compassionate or merciful. The concept T.S. Eliot used in his poem The Waste Land as the suggestion of thunder. He took it from the Upanishads where it means compassion.

Dazzling darkness   This term appears now and then in relation to fantastic mystical experiences in different writings.

Dearth   Lack, often severe.

Dee, John (1527-1608)   Magician, astronomer, astrologer, mathematician. The reference here is to Theorem 11 of Monas Hieroglyphica (1564).

Demeter   Goddess of harvest in Greek myth.

Destiny   The purpose to which someone is appointed, the inevitable.

Deus (Latin)   God.

Devekut (Hebrew)   Dedication or clinging to God.

Dharma (Sanskrit)   Good conduct.

Dhyana (Sanskrit)   Contemplation, reflection and meditation. Origin of words chan and zen supposedly.

Discord   The opposite of accord, also a concept in quantum physics.

Diversion   Changing course, amusing, or re-directing attention.

Divination   Seeking to know the future, finding hidden things.

Divinization   To treat as divine.

Djed (Egyptian)   Symbol of a pillar, said to be the spine of Osiris.

DMT   N, N-Dimethyltryptamine. Hallucinogenic, psychoactive naturally occurring substance.

Doldrums   Area where calm and strange winds prevail, a period of low spirits.

Druid   Magician or priest among the Celts.

Dumb   The meaning here is silent.

Duomo (Italian)   Cathedral, and here a reference to Brunelleschi's Duomo in Florence.

Dyeus   The 're-constructed' ancient Indo-European god.

Eavesdropping   Listening secretly, under the eaves.

Ecsomatic   A term for out-of-body movement.

Eerie   Weird, strange and frightening.

Efflorescence   State of flowering.

Egest   To expel from the body.

Ego   The self, conscious and thinking.

Egocentric   Self-centredness.

Egoist   Person who concentrates too much on themselves.

Egotist   Conceited.

Egress   Act of going out.

Eldorado (Spanish)   The golden one.

Emerson, Ralph Waldo (1803-1882)   US poet and leader of transcendentalist movement.

Empiricism   Relying of experience and experiments.

Encompass   It commonly means to encircle although it has older meanings.

Ennui   Boredom.

Enochian   Angel language of John Dee.

Entanglement   Also used as a key concept in quantum physics.

Entheogen   A psychoactive substance generating the divine within.

Enthrall   To hold spellbound, to fascinate.

Entropy   Measure of unavailable energy and a process of degradation.

Ephemeral   Fleeting.

Epiphanies   Sudden, spiritual revelations or realisations, often divine.

Equilibrioception   The sense of balance.

Ere   Before.

Eros   Greek god of love.

Esoteric   Unusual, understood by a small group of people. Esoterica is the noun.

Ether   The clear, upper air, an all embracing medium for waves, from the Greek words for the heavens and to light up, similarly ethereal. Also etheric.

Etherised   Anesthetised.

Et tu (Latin) 'And you,' as in 'Et tu Brute' from Julius Caesar by Shakespeare.

Eudaemonia (Greek) Ethics looking at happiness as a test, from the Greek word for well and spirit.

Evelyn Underhill (1875-1941) Her book *Mysticism* in 1911 survives very well. Philosopher, teacher.

Evensong Evening prayer of song in the Anglican community.

Excrescence Outgrowth or projection.

Exitus Departure, exit, death.

Ex libris (Latin) Out of the book.

Exsufflation Blowing out of air, or force of expiration of air.

Familiar Well known, friendly, on a family basis, acquainted with but also the demon spirit used by a witch.

Far (Swedish) Father.

Fashed Troubled.

Fata Morgana An optical illusion at horizons, often at sea.

Faun Half human, half goat mythic creature.

Ficino, Marsilio (1433-1499) Priest, scholar, philosopher, astrologer. He was a significant figure in the Renaissance and sought to reconcile Platonic and Christian thought.

Fisher King Myth of the Fisher King who was injured and needs to be healed, whose impotence caused a wasteland, involving Percival or Parzival amongst others.

Flail A tool for threshing.

Flume A channel of water downhill usually to transport materials.

Flying Dutchman A legendary ghost ship.

Fortune Chance, luck, destiny, wealth.

Foundered Sunk.

Fountainhead The source, the beginning.

Fractal Geometric pattern generated by repeating.

Fravarti Angel of lights in Zorastrianism.

Gauge Measure.

Gauze Type of weave, medical material to cover wounds.

Genius Exceptional creative or intellectual power or person but also a spirit presiding over a person or place.

Gens People, from Latin.

Genus Class, kind, group.

Glamour Apart from its standard meaning it also refers to magic and enchantment.

Gnomes Means both mythic sprite and also a pithy saying that may be in verse.

Gnosis Knowledge of a spiritual nature.

Golden Bough, The The influential book that became *The Golden Bough: A Study in Magic and Religion* was written by James George Frazer. His long journey and thesis began because of his curiosity about the incident of the Golden Bough in the Aeneid.

Golem Figure brought to life by magic, robot in Jewish writings.

Gonad Reproductive gland.

Gospel of Mary Apocryphal book discovered in 1896 and dated to early Christian times.

Gospel of St. Thomas Non-canonical Gospel discovered in 1945.

Gossamer Fine spider silk.

Great Crested Grebe This water bird is also a great swimmer and diver.

Great Seeking Sometimes appearing in esoteric studies, or alchemy.

Great Spirit Native American concept of God.

Greyson, Bruce Professor of psychiatry. Expert in NDEs.

Griffiths Roland Professor researching mood-altering drugs and mystical experiences.

Grimoire Magic text book, book of spells. Believed to be related to the word grammar.

Gyre Circle, or spiral turn.

Haiku Japanese form of poetry based on seventeen syllables.

Hail To greet or to come from.

Hall, Manly Palmer (1901-1990) Writer of *The Secret Teachings of all the Ages* (1928).

Hallelujah Meaning praise God or as an expression of joy.

Hallow Holy person or object.

Halo Ring of light around a holy person or an object.

Halyard Rope for hoisting a sail.

Hara Soft belly, dantian.

Hard Problem of Consciousness This is the difficulty explaining why sentient beings have phenomenal experiences.

Harris Rachel Psychotherapist who has written *Listening to Ayahuasca*.

Hashed Jumbled, mixed, mangled.

Hawking, Stephen (1942-2018) Theoretical physicist. He identified that AI was an existential threat to humans.

"He does not see through the soul.." *Gospel of Mary*.

Heavenly Heart The pineal gland or pituitary.

Heaven Seventeen Name of a band in *A Clockwork Orange* that was used by British band 'Heaven 17.'

Heka (Egyptian) The word has a number of references from the god of magic to the practice thereof. It seems to have been unduly narrowed to refer to 'Egyptian Witchcraft.'

Hence From here and also from the living.

Henosis Greek word for mystical union.

Here be Dragons A reference to mythological features associated with unknown regions appearing on ancient maps.

Hermetic Related to Hermes the Thrice Great, Hermes Trismegistus supposed author of the Hermetic Corpus.

Hesychasm Quiet prayer contemplation often used in early Christianity.

Hex Magic spell or curse.

Hildegard de Bingen, St. (1098-1179) Great German mystic.

Hof, Wim 'The Ice Man' developer of the Wim Hof Method.

Hogwash Refuse for hogs, nonsense.

Holy Grail Legend associated with Perceval the Fisher King.

Hoo This is a sound used in a number of meditative or spiritual practices.

Hoodoo Bewitching, bringing bad luck.

Hopkins, Gerard Manley (1844-1899) Jesuit, poet, inventor of sprung rhythm. Born in England he was sent to Ireland and was incredibly unhappy there. His vision and reality were very far apart.

Houdini, Harry (1874-1926) Magician who exposed false spiritualism.

Hu Often used as a mantra. Ancient name for God.

Hubris Arrogance inviting disaster.

Hunt in the Forest The celebrated painting by Uccello, circa 1470. Also known as The Hunt by Night, The Hunt.

Huxley, Aldous (1894-1963) Student of mysticism, Perennial Philosophy, author of *Brave New World* among many books.

Hypnogogic The state before falling asleep. Also spelt hypnagogic.

Hypnopompic Waking up state.

Ib One spelling of heart in Ancient Egypt.

Icarus Son of Daedalus who flew too high against warnings.

I Ching Ancient Chinese divination book tool.

Id Unconscious mass of primitive energies.

Idealism Reality is mental or immaterial.

'I forgive all human beings....' Variant of Jainist prayer.

Imago Mature, often winged stage of the insect or ideal mental image of someone.

Imbued Filled, inspired.

Immanent Dwelling within, pervading.

Immerging Plunging, immersing.

Immersing Plunged in water or being deep in something.

Imminent Impending.

Immingling To mingle together.

Immiscible Not capable of being mixed.

Immit To insert, to infuse.

Immixed To mix, commingle.

Imp Usually small mischievous demons or mythological creatures.

Imperium Absolute sovereignty.

Imperturbability Calm, incapable of being upset.

Imposture Act of deception using identity.

Incandescent Glowing brightly or white hot.

Incarceration Putting in a prison or enclosure or confining.

Incommensurate Inadequate, disproportionate.

Individuated Associated with individuation which is a key concept for Carl Jung.

Indra's net Mythic net of the god Indra with jewel at each vertex.

Ineffable Cannot be uttered or described.

Infinite Way, The A book and universal, spiritual approach by Joel S. Goldsmith (1892-1964).

Infusione (Italian) Infusion.

Inglenook (Scots) Alcove to sit in a hearth.

Inklings Hints, intimations, also a group of fantasy writers in Oxford including C.S Lewis, Charles Williams and Tolkien.

Instantiates Provides an example of and thereby attests.

Instress Gerard Manley Hopkins' term for the force or energy which sustains an inscape.

Insufflation Act of blowing something into the human body.

Interfluent Flowing between.

Internuncio Messenger between two parties.

"In the beginning..." *King James Bible*, John 1:1.

Intussusception Drawing in of something from without. Telescoping of part of a tube in another.

Inured Hardened in or habituated.

Involution Here used in the sense of degeneration.

Ire Anger.

Iridescent Coloured like a rainbow or showing different colours from different angles.

Ishvara (Sanskrit) Many meanings from God to soul.

"It droppeth.." Portia in *The Merchant of Venice,* Act 4, Scene 1.

Jacaranda Tropical tree regarded as sacred by some.

Jack o' Lantern Jack of the lantern, a ghost light.

Jacob's Ladder Ladder dreamt of by Jacob connecting to God.

Jeopardy Hazard or danger from Latin and French meaning of divided game.

Judo Martial art meaning 'the gentle way.'

Ju-jitsu Japanese martial art meaning the art of yielding.

Jung, Carl (1875-1961) Psychiatrist and psychologist.

Ka Part of the soul in Ancient Egyptian conception.

Kaaba Sacred site in Mecca.

Ka ba ankh Egyptian symbol.

Kabbalah Jewish mystical tradition also Kabbala and other spellings.

Kama Desire, longing.

Kamala (Sanskrit) Meaning lotus, may be used in relation to deities.

Kami Object of worship or divine being in Shinto in Japan.

Kano, Jigoro (1860-1938) Founder of judo, educator.

Kaon A subatomic particle.

Karma Spiritual principle of cause and effect.

Kashmir Shaivism Non-dualist Tantric tradition.

Katharsis Greek origin of word catharsis in English.

Keep The most protected part of a castle.

Keller, Helen (1880-1968) Author and activist.

Kenosis The emptying of will to become receptive to divine will in Christianity.

Kevala Jnana (Sanskrit) Jainism omniscience.

Kierkegaard, Sören (1813-1855) Danish philosopher.

Koan Confusing questions to meditate upon in Zen Buddhism.

Kukulkan Mayan snake god, recurring South American god also an individual.

Kundalini Type of primal energy located at base of spine that can be awakened for higher powers.

Language Instinct, The Phrase most often associated with Steven Pinker's book of that name suggesting an innate capacity for language in humans.

Lantern of Osiris Sometimes used as a description of the ancient Egyptian representation of the spiritual eye.

Law of Attraction A concept in New Thought and a book by Abraham-Hicks.

Laudanum Tincture of opium.

Lectio (Latin) Reading.

Lewis C.S. (1898-1963) Taught at Oxford, writer of *The Chronicles of Narnia* and many others.

Libra Scales, seventh sign of zodiac.

Liminal On the threshold, also refers to the middle stage of a ritual.

Lodestar A star that leads or guides or inspires.

Lodge A body of masons or a place where certain societies met or a small building.

Logia Sayings, especially those of Christ.

Logodaedulus A person skilled in the manipulative use of words.

Logogriph Riddle where words are found from other words made up of its letters.

Logos Active principle determining the world, Word of God.

Loki Norse evil god.

'Love many trust few...' A saying that seems to originate somewhere in the US over a hundred and fifty years ago.

Lucas, George Filmmaker behind Star Wars.

Lugh Warrior, king, god in Irish mythology.

Luke   The biggest contributor to the New Testament according to some. Name of protoganist in *Star Wars*.

Lumbered   Encumbered.

Lumen (Latin)   Means light but also in English means amongst other things the cavity of a tubular origin. Luminous also means enlightening.

Lustre   Sheen or shine but it was also a Roman purification ceremony.

Lux (Latin)   Word for light.

Ma   Japanese concept of negative space. Also common word for mother.

Maban   Aboriginal term for life force.

Macbeth   Shakespeare's play, written circa 1600 is still full of dark power.

Magenta   Mixture of red and blue, that appears purple or pink or a mixture thereof, not occurring in the visible spectrum.

Magic Flute, The   Opera by Mozart that premiered in 1791, full of esoteric symbolism.

Magicicada   Genus of the periodical cicadas.

Magnetoception   Sense of magnetism.

Magnus Opus (Latin)   Great work.

Mahatma   A wise person or great soul.

Mail   Post and also armour.

Mana   Supernatural, spiritual quality in certain Pacific cultures.

Mandala   Picture symbol of universe for spiritual uses.

Manifold   Meaning both many and a topological space like our universe perhaps.

Manitou   Spirit concept of certain North American native peoples.

Manna   Divinely inspired spiritual nourishment, the food that fell for the Israelites in the desert.

Mantra   Sacred or numinous sound or syllables for spiritual uses in meditation and prayer.

Maslow, Abraham (1908-1970)   He studied motivation and personality.

Matrix   The place in which something is formed.

Maya   Amongst many meanings, a concealing factor in Buddhist thought.

Mayhap Old word for perhaps.

Mayhem Chaos.

Mazda Ahuru Zoroastrian God.

Mazard Head or skull.

Meditatio (Latin) Meditation.

Mercury Messenger of the gods, identified with Hermes, also the silvery metallic element known as quicksilver.

Merkaba (Hebrew) Chariot associated with concepts of mysticism, school of Jewish mysticism also Merkabah.

Mesmerism Sometimes used instead of hypnotism after Franz Mesmer (1734-1815).

Metaphysical This usually refers to philosophy or poetry that deals with abstract issues associated with existence and the realm beyond the perceptible.

Michael Archangel, a healing and protective symbol across the monotheistic world, whose name means 'Who is like God.'

Microtubules Microscopic tubular structures in cells.

Midas Greek king whose touch turned everything to gold.

Middle Pillar The central pillar of the tree of life, associated with magic and spiritual rituals.

Milky Way The galaxy where our solar system is, from the Latin Via Lactea.

Minotaur The bull monster in the labyrinth in Crete.

Miranda Prospero's daughter in Shakespeare's *The Tempest*.

Mirandola, Giovanni Pico della (1463-1494) Renaissance philosopher.

Moksha Freedom from samsara, spiritual liberation.

Monad Multiple meaning but usually a symbol of a complete being, spirit or God represented by a point in a circle. One, unit.

Monism Emphasises the oneness of a concept.

Moody, Raymond Philosopher and psychologist.

Mukti See moksha above.

Muppets   Puppets created by Jim Henson and Jane Henson in 1955.

Murphy, Todd   Neurotheologist.

Mystagogue   The definition is given in the line where it appears.

Mystery Religions   Religions of the Greco-Roman world involving voluntary initiation.

Mysticism   From the word to conceal in Greek, it refers to a recurrent practice, phenomenon, experience of individuals seeking a higher state of being. As defined in the Gateway.

Nadir   The lowest point of anything

Naos   Inner cell of a temple.

Narcissus   Greek myth associated with falling in love with own image.

NDE   Near Death Experience term used by Raymond Moody but the phenomenon is recorded for hundreds of years.

Neshamah (Hebrew)   Breath also synonym for spirit.

Netherworld   The underworld.

New Atheism   Also called fundamental atheism by some.

Newberg, Andrew   Researcher into neurotheology who co-wrote *How God Changes your Brain*.

Newgrange   Prehistoric monument in Ireland circa 5,000 years old. On the Winter Solstice, the sun shines into the inner chamber.

New Thought Movement   19th century movement in the US spearheaded by Phineas Quimby (1802-1866) source of the Law of Attraction linked to mind cures, paralleling Christian Science.

Nexus   A bond.

Nirvana (Sanskrit)   Blissful state or cessation of existence, from the words blown out. High state of Buddhism.

NLP   Neuro-linguistic programming.

Nociception   The sense of pain.

Non-local consciousness   Idea that consciousness is not confined to the brain.

Noumenon Once contrasted with phenomenon, objects of highest knowledge. Unknowable. Term used by Kant.

Numen Latin term that came to mean divine presence.

Obelisk Tall pillar with pyramid on top, found particularly in ancient Egypt and spread therefrom.

Objectivism Philosophy of Ayn Rand.

Objectivity Focusing on the external, practical, observed, exterior to mind.

Obloquy Censure, slander, to speak against.

Obsequies Funeral rites.

Obsequious Compliant, fawning.

Occult Simply meant hidden, but refers to a range of esoteric practices that include magic, alchemy, religion.

Oculus Round window.

Oedipus In the Greek myth, Oedipus killed his father King Laius unbeknownst to him at the time after which he married his mother Queen Jocasta who would kill herself and he blinds himself.

Om (Sanskrit) Sacred sound of universe, often written 'aum.'

One Ring, The Symbol from *The Lord of the Rings*.

Opal Precious stone often used as a symbol.

Oracle Medium of divine revelation.

Orangutan Asian great ape found in Borneo, meaning person of the forest.

Osiris Great Egyptian god, of afterlife, resurrection.

Ouroboros Symbol of serpent with tail in its mouth, representing completion.

Padma The sacred lotus.

Paeon Physician of the gods.

Palimpsest Manuscript where former writing has been over-written.

Pallas Athena Greek goddess of wisdom.

Panacea Something providing a cure for everything.

Pandemonium Craziness, tumultuous uproar (with the word 'demon' in it).

Pandora's Box   The box opened that released ills in human life in Greek myth.

Pantheism   Often associated with Spinoza. The worship of all gods. Reality identified with divinity. Sees universe as manifesting God.

Pantheon   The temple of all the gods in Rome, open at the top to the elements.

Parallax   Changing perspective based on changed viewing position.

Parasomatic   Experiencing that you are in a different body.

Patanjali   Author or compiler of the celebrated Yoga Sutras.

Patriarch   Ruling father.

Patternicity   Evolutionary tendency to find patterns even where they do not exist.

Pavilion   As well as being a building this also refers to certain places and states in the body, particularly in Taoist writings.

Pawned   To pledge, to give as security.

Pearlescent   Having the gloss of a pearl. The pearl is often a spiritual symbol.

"..Pentecost.."   From Acts 2, *King James Bible*, describing the coming of the Holy Spirit.

Perdition   Loss or ruin.

Peregrination   Wandering.

Perennial   Enduring, recurrent.

Perennial Philosophy   A philosophy which sees a central, common source or truth in all or much spiritual, esoteric and exoteric endeavours despite apparent diversity.

Periphery   Boundary, from the Greek meaning to carry around.

Perpetual   Everlasting.

Persephone   Greek daughter of Zeus and queen of the underworld.

Personal pronoun   Word which stands for a definite person or thing.

Pert   Exuberant is one meaning.

Peterson, Jordan   Contemporary psychologist and author.

Phantasmagoria Fantastic assembly of appearances.

Phenomenology In psychology, the study of the structure of consciousness through subjective experience associated with Husserl and others.

Philip K. Dick (1928-1982) Great science fiction writer. The book *The Exegesis of Philip K. Dick* represents a remarkable metaphysical exploration.

Philosopher's stone Imaginary stone sought by alchemists to turn base metal into gold, often symbol for soul.

Phoebus Greek sun god, Apollo.

Phoenix Mythical bird that rises from the ashes, reborn or renewed.

Pinhole Pinholes were long used for optical devices such as pinhole cameras.

Placebo A fake medicine which nevertheless produces an effect.

Planck, Max (1858-1947) Theoretical physicist.

Plato (circa 427-347 B.C.) Great Greek philosopher.

Plenar Entire, absolute.

Plenipotentiary Someone with full powers.

Plenum Full space of group.

Pleroma Fullness, with various esoteric meanings for the Gnostics and others such as the totality of divine powers.

Plethora Abundance or fullness.

Plosive Release of breath after stoppage to make consonant sounds.

Pneumatics These were the highest orders of humans for Gnostics.

Pontiff Pope. Bridge builder according to one view.

Portent Sign or omen.

Posterity Future generations.

Postulant Candidate for a religious or monastic order, someone who asks.

Potentate Powerful ruler.

Prakriti (Sanskrit) Primal matter, feminine force.

Prana (Sanskrit) Word for breath of life.

Predicate Something stated about a proposition or a foundation.

Prelapsarian Of the time of innocence before the Fall in theology.

Premier First, earliest.

Premium Superior quality, reward.

Preposition Small words showing relationships.

Prepossessing Attractive, possessing beforehand.

Prequel A story which precedes an earlier.

Presentiment A feeling that something is going to happen.

Presentment Presenting to view or consciousness.

Preside To rule, occupy place of authority.

Preternatural Extraordinary, inexplicable, beyond nature.

Prim Stiff, precise, proper.

Primal From an early stage in evolutionary development, fundamental.

Primary First.

Primate Order of mammals, religious leader.

Primeval Relating to the earliest stages in human history.

Priming Prepared for, conditioning in a psychological sense.

Primitive Basic or early stage of evolution.

Primordial Existing from the start.

Principal Chief, most important.

Principality Territory of a prince or one of the orders of angels.

Prisca Theologia Meaning ancient theology associated with Marsilio
    Ficino (1433-1499).

Prissy Fussy, respectable.

Pristine Pure, relating to the earliest condition.

Prius Something which is prior and takes precedence.

Proboscis Elongated appendage usually from the head.

Prodigy Amazing or unusual person, developed very young.

Promised land The Biblical term also has a more symbolic meaning.

Propagating Travel through space, extend, foster.

Prophet One who is contacted by divine forces to communicate or one
    who foretells.

Proprioception The sense of position of body parts.

Prospero Magician in Shakespeare's *The Tempest*.

Protagonist Chief actor, main character.

Protean Able to change easily.

Protoplasm The theological meaning of first formed was taken over by science.

Prototype The first or original type.

Providence Meaning foresight, although its sense of divine providence has become more common.

Psilocybin Hallucinogenic mushrooms.

Psyche Soul, spirit or mind. In Greek myth, Psyche falls in love with Cupid or Eros.

Psychedelic Relaxed state of the higher mental powers from word for the Greek word mind and to reveal or make visible. The word exists independently of the drug-induced context.

Psychics This refers to people claiming extra-sensory perception. It also seems to be historically set against 'pneumatics' to distinguish types of seekers with powers. In Buddhism, seekers can obtain higher powers through seeking as yoga also promises.

Purusha (Sanskrit) Can mean the unchanging spirit, universal force, although it has multiple uses.

Pyrrhic victory This is a victory whose price is ruinous or tantamount to defeat.

Pythagoras (570-495 BC) Mystic, mathematician, associated with mystery religion.

Quantum coherence Refers to a property associated with waves, applied in quantum theory and utilised very rarely in relation to discussion of the soul actually or metaphorically.

Quicksilver Mercury.

Quintessence The fifth essence or the pure essence.

Qui vive (French) Who lives? Who goes there?

Quo vadis (Latin) Where are you going?

Ra   Sun god in ancient Egypt.

Rahman   One of the names of God in Islam.

Rainbow Bridge   This occurs in mythology and esoterica, for example in Norse mythology, linking earth to the realm of the gods or Asgard.

Rajah (Sanskrit)   Attribute or tendency towards activity.

Rama (Sanskrit)   An incarnation of Vishnu.

Rand Ayn (1905-1982)   Russian writer and philosopher.

Raphael   Archangel associated with healing.

Rasputin, Grigorij (1869-1916)   Russian mystic.

Ratzon l-kabel (Hebrew)   Desire to receive.

Ray   Ray of creation.

Rebus   Representation of a word using pictures, riddle.

Recur   To happen again regularly.

Recure   To heal.

Red crown of Egypt   This was called the Deshret, never found but often depicted.

Reditus (Latin)   A return.

Regiratio   Return, with specific meaning in Christian theology.

Rejuvenescent   Renewing youth.

Remote-viewing   Attempting to view places without use of technology or being present.

Reoccur   To occur again but not as regularly as recurring.

Replevin   A legal claim for possession.

Reveille   Waking call.

Reverie   Often undirected thought or daydream.

Ring, Kenneth   Author of *The Omega Project: Near Death Experiences, UFO Encounters and Mind at Large*.

Romantic   Emphasising the subjective, heroic, daring.

Ruah (Hebrew)   Signifying divine breath or spirit.

Rubicon   The point of no turning back, based on Caesar's crossing of the river of that name leading to the Roman civil war.

Rumi (1207-1273) Persian mystic and poet.

Rune Meant a secret or mystery then became magic symbols and then the Scandinavian early script.

Sacerdotal Associated with a priesthood.

Sackcloth and ashes Practice and symbol of repentance.

Sacrum Where the spine connects to the pelvis also known as the holy bone and linked to kundalini.

Sadhana (Sanskrit) Spiritual practice repeated to gain spiritual perfection.

Sahaja (Sanskrit) Natural, co-emergent.

Sahaja samadhi (Sanskrit) May be used sometimes as a very high state of awareness combined with functionality in other domains.

Sahasrara (Sanskrit) Crown chakra.

Sain To make the sign of the cross over, to heal.

Samadhi (Sanskrit) State of high awareness.

Samhain (Irish) Celtic festival of a liminal time that was origins of Halloween and other Christian spiritual celebrations.

Samsara (Sanskrit) Cycle of birth, rebirth.

Samyama (Sanskrit) Very high level of awareness produced by meditation.

Sanctum A holy site, part of a temple where deities are present.

Sapentia (Latin) Wisdom. May be higher than scientia (knowledge). Sapience is the English derivation and of course we are Homo Sapiens.

Sarah Wife of Abraham.

Saraha 8th to 9th century Buddhist teacher.

Saraswati Hindu goddess.

Satanism The worship of Satan.

Satchitananda (Sanskrit) Subjective experience of absolute reality, true, conscious, bliss.

Satori Zen concept associated with ultimate realisation of the nature of things.

Sattva (Sanskrit) The attribute or tendency towards truth, positivity, wholesomeness.

Satyagraha (Sanskrit)   Gandhi's doctrine based on the concepts of truth and force.

Satyr   Lustful male figures or spirits in Greek mythology, gods of the woodlands.

Scala (Latin)   Ladder. This was often a divine ladder as for example in *The Ladder of Divine Ascent* from 600 A.D.

'Scent of the Rose-Garden reached thee and thou didst go to the Rose-Garden.'   This is a line from Rumi from *The Works of Shams of Tabriz*.

Schumann frequency   Global electromagnetic resonance phenomenon.

Scientism   The ideology promoting science as the fundamental answer.

Scintilla   A very small amount, spark.

Scylla and Charbydis   Mythical sea monsters in Greek legend representing two evils that had to be navigated.

Sea of Tranquility   Geological formation on the moon, and an acupressure point on the body.

Secede   To draw apart.

Second brain   Enteric nervous system. Neurons in the intestine that act independently, often seen as significant in traditional conceptions of health.

Secret of the Golden Flower, The   Chinese Taoist classic.

Seity   Selfhood.

Self-effacing   Humble, staying in background.

Sem (Tibetan)   Part of concept of self.

Sentience   The capacity to feel, experience subjectively, from the Latin word for feeling.

Sequestered   To set aside, to set apart.

Sere   Dry and withered.

Setanta   Cuchulainn's younger self.

Seth Material, The   Jane Roberts book that is associated with New Age.

Seventeenth of Tammuz An important date in Judaism, remembering a series of unfortunate events in their history including Moses smashing the Ten Commandments after finding the Golden Calf.

Seventh Heaven In some religious and esoteric heavens the highest heaven.

Shakespeare (1564-1616) The quote is from Sonnet 17. *The Tempest* is also referred to below as is *Macbeth*.

Shakti (Sanskrit) Goddess. A supreme, feminine force or being in Indian tradition.

Shaman Spirit or medicine person or priest in traditional societies.

Shamash Mesopotamian sun god.

Shamayim (Hebrew) Heaven.

Sheldrake, Rupert Contemporary biologist interested in spirituality.

Shemash (Hebrew) Sun.

Shen Chinese concept of the divine spirit or spirit.

Shiva Indian God with different emphasis in different traditions.

Shook foil Phrase used by Gerard Manley Hopkins in the poem *God's Grandeur*.

Short shrift Short time for confession before execution, summary treatment.

Sibilant The hissing, soft sound caused by certain syllables.

Siddharta Birth name of founder of Buddhism.

Siddhi (Sanskrit) Supernatural powers that come from spiritual perfection of meditation.

Sidhe Supernatural race in Irish mythology. Aos sí, people of the mounds.

Sigil Magic symbol.

Signature The doctrine of signatures involved the idea that the uses of plants was indicated in their appearance, usually as a divine gift.

Silkie (Scots) Also Selkie. Seal folk.

Silver cord Link between aspect of spirit body and physical body.

Singularity   The elusive concept that seems to mutate regularly and often now refers to a coming event or point or condition of technological evolution and usually involving machine 'intelligence' passing humankind.

Sirely   An old spelling of 'surly' meaning bad tempered, with the former containing the word 'sir.'

Skillion   A lean-to house, outbuilding.

Skilly   Thin gruel.

Smith, Huston (1919-2016)   Religious scholar.

"So no one says…"   *Gospel of Mary.*

Solfeggio   Use of syllables sung to notes of scale.

Sonata   Classical form of musical instrumental composition usually in three movements.

Sophia   Concept or goddess or wisdom.

Sophia perennis (Latin)   Perennial wisdom.

Sophrosyne   Greek concept of self-control as a foundation for higher virtues.

Soporific   Dulling awareness, sleep inducing.

Sorcery   Enchantment, magic, witchcraft, use of evil spirits.

Soul   I use the word soul infrequently. Sometimes the word is used by others as synonymous with spirit, sometimes not. There is a distinction in special contexts.

Source, The   Often used as a synonym for divine force or universal force.

Space Elevator   Technology foreseen to lift humans directly into space.

Spiritoso   Instruction in music, play with spirit.

Spiritus   A spirit, a breathing.

Spooky action   Einstein famously used the phrase 'spooky action at a distance' in the context of discussions on the quantum world.

Sprite   Certain legendary figures such as elves.

Star Chamber   Secret court in England starting in the Late Middle Ages that ultimately became oppressive.

Stargate Sometimes a science fiction idea of a portal for travel through space and time.

Star Trek Cult TV series from USA. The teleportation device was an important one therein.

Stash Secret store.

Stein, Edith (1891-1942) Great Jewish-Catholic Theologian, student of Husserl.

Still Quiet, single frame, device for distilling.

Stymie To thwart.

Sublimated Transforming a base emotion to higher or changing a solid to a gas.

Sublime Majestic, awe creating, exalted.

Sufism Main type of Islamic mysticism.

Sum Total or in Latin 'I am.'

Sump A pit or depression into which water drains as in a mine.

Sumph Stupid person, may be surly.

Sumpter Packhorse.

Sunyata (Sanskrit) Buddhist concept of emptinesss or empty awareness.

Superaltar Stone used as a temporary altar.

Supercoil Complex coil of proteins or DNA.

Superconsciousness This is a description by some of the highest form of awareness available to us.

Superessence An essence above the normal, traceable at least back to Eriugena and early Christian and mystical writers.

Supernal Heavenly.

Surcease Cease.

Surly Bad-tempered, old spelling 'sirly.'

Suscipient One who receives a sacrament.

Sushumna (Sanskrit) Energy channel that goes up the spine or parallel thereto.

Susurration Whisper or whispering sounds.

Sutra (Sanskrit) An aphoristic rule.

Sutrama (Sanskrit) Silver cord, described as energy filaments linking astral body with physical one.

Sweat lodge Often used in the vision quest of Native Americans and seeker which may lead to experiences similar to out of body ones. Sometimes written as one word 'sweatlodge.'

Swedenborg, Emanuel (1688-1772) Swedish polymath, philosopher, theologian, scientist, mystic.

Synchronicity Carl Jung's concept of meaningful coincidences.

Syncretise Fusion of ideas or religions.

Tabernacle Dwelling place, tent, place to hold sacred substance or meeting.

Tai-chi Chinese system of self defence and exercise utilising chi.

'Take..' no part in fruitless works of evil..' Ephesians 5:11.

Tallow Animal fat used for making candles.

Tamas (Sanskrit) Attribute of darkness.

Tantulus Son of Zeus punished by being placed in water.

Tao Absolute entity source of existence and change. Philosophical or spiritual tradition focusing on understanding the Tao. Also Dao.

Tara Hindu goddess, sacred place in Ireland.

Tare A weed that looks like corn.

Tathagatha (Sanskrit) It can mean true reality or self, but certainly indicates a high level of detachment so that the Buddha could use it about himself.

Te Virtuous power in Chinese philosophy.

Technocracy Technocrats in control of us.

Technos Here used as a name for the religion that worship technology.

Telestrion Initiation hall in Eleusis in ancient Greece.

Tempest, The Shakespeare's play written circa 1610.

Ten Bulls Also the Ten Ox Herding pictures from the meditation practices of Zen Buddhism. Dating from 12th century China.

Terah Father of Abraham.

Tesla's coil Electrical resonant, transformer circuit invented by Nikola Tesla.

Tet (Egyptian) Spelt different ways, known as the knot of Isis.

Tetragrammaton Biblical name of God.

Theophanic Appearance or manifestation of deity to people.

Theoria (Greek) Refers to a knowing through seeing, often as contemplation in Christianity.

Theos (Greek) A god.

Theosis Seeking change through union with God.

Theta Eighth letter of the Greek alphabet and a type of brain wave.

Thich Quang Duc (1987-1963) The burning monk.

Three Forms of First Thought One of the Gnostic Gospels in the Nag Hammadi documents discovered in 1945.

Thor The god of thunder in Scandinavian mythology.

Thoreau, Henry David (1817-1862) Writer, naturalist, transcendentalist.

Thoth Egyptian god of art and science.

Tinder Material used for lighting a fire.

'Toora loora loora, toora loora li...' Irish American popular song written in 1913 and made famous again by Bing Crosby.

Tor Rocky outcrop, often with sacred significance e.g Glastonbury Tor.

Torpedoed Destroyed.

Torus Figure or shape generated by revolution of a circle around a straight line.

Transcendentalism The state of being transcendental, the school of thought associated with Ralph Waldon Emerson and others in the early decades of the 19th century in the USA. It emphasises the individual and intuition as against institutions and may be seen as Romantic. It influenced the New Thought movement in the USA.

Transhumanism Moving towards man-machine merger.

Transitus The passage through death in Christianity.

Transpersonal Psychology   Domain building on James, Assagioli, Maslow, Grof, Krippner, Tart, Wilber and many others.

Trans-subjective   Looking to commonality incorporating the subjective and beyond.

Tree of life   Various uses from Darwin across a range of archetypal descriptions often associated with sacred trees.

Trickster   A mythical or archetypal being with special knowledge who operates through playing tricks or games.

Trifles   Things of little value.

Trinkets   Ornaments of little value.

True light   'The true light that gave light to everyone was coming into the world.' John 1:9.

Turing Test   Developed by Alan Turing to test a machine's ability to communicate like humans.

Turtle Dove   Type of dove often a symbol of innocence.

Tympanum   Space between the lintel or doorway and the arch in a cathedral and also the middle ear.

Uccello, Paolo (1397-1475)   Painter, pioneer in perspective, mathematician.

Unbeknownst   Meaning not known to someone.

Unbrutish   Used here as an opposite of brutish, which means coarse, inhuman, like lower animals.

Unio Mystica (Latin)   Mystical union.

Universal Grammar   Theory of universal grammar is associated with Noam Chomsky, positing an innate set of grammar rules.

Ur   Meaning original but also in a secondary sense is used as text for 'your' or 'you're.'

Uraeus   Ancient Egyptian cobra symbol on forehead of Pharaoh crown.

Ushnisha   The shape on the crown of the Buddha, symbolising spiritual connection for some.

Ut (Latin)   As, so, that, when. Formerly the first musical note of a hexachord also abbreviation for universal time.

VALIS This was the concept and book by Philip K. Dick and stands for Vast Active Living Intelligence System.

Van Dusen, Wilson (1923-2005) Psychologist and author.

Van Gogh, Vincent (1853-1890) The Potato Eaters represented a level in Van Gogh's work and the Sunflowers series a yet higher one on the artistic, evolutionary path.

Van Lommel, Pim (born 1943) Cardiologist and author of study on NDEs.

Vassal Dependant or slave.

Vedanta Hindu philosophy based on the Upanishads.

Vertex Crown of the head, top of summit.

Vesica Piscis Shape formed by intersection of two circles, representing many things from a glory to Christ.

Vestibule Entrance court, antechamber.

Virgo The Virgin, the sixth sign of the zodiac.

Void, The This has been used as a description of the peaceful emptiness encountered through mystical practices and elsewhere.

Vortex Flow rotating around an axis. Whirling mass in spiral.

VR Virtual Reality.

Wa (Japanese) Harmony.

Waste Land, The Poem written in 1922 by T.S. Eliot (1888-1965).

Watan Tanka (Lakota) Divine, Great Spirit, Great Mystery.

Weir A horizontal barrier across a river.

Weird This word meant more than just odd, but also having power over destiny.

Whence From where.

Whitman, Walt (1819-1892) Poet.

"Wholly on heavenly things…" Line from John Donne's (1572-1631) *Holy Sonnet 17*.

Wigwam Tent used by Native Americans, often made from birch bark.

William James (1842-1910) Philosopher, psychologist, physician, pragmatist.

Will o' the wisp Hovering light over marshy ground, a thing difficult to catch.

Winnow Getting rid of something such as chaff often using air.

Wizard A man with magical powers.

Wordsworth, William (1770-1850) English poet interested in mysticism.

Worrycow A frightening creature.

Wotan German name for god Woden.

Yeats, William Butler (1865-1939) Irish poet, playwright, Senator and member of the the Order of the Golden Dawn.

Yin-yang The Chinese and oriental philosophy of complementary duality.

Yonder Far over there.

Zen The Japanese branch of Buddhism allowing enlightenment to be found through self-mastery.

Zenith The greatest height or the point of the celestial sphere above your head.

Ziggurat Ancient Mesopotamian tower or temple.

About the Author

James Tunney obtained an honours degree in law from Trinity College Dublin, qualified as a Barrister at the Honorable Society of the King's Inn, Dublin and obtained an LLM from Queen Mary College, University of London.

Since then he worked as a Lecturer and Senior Lecturer in UK universities. He has been a Visiting Professor in Germany and France, lecturer around the world and worked as an international legal consultant in places such as Lesotho and Moldova for bodies such as the UNDP. He talked in many countries and published regularly on issues associated with globalisation. He has taught, written and talked about subjects such as indigenous rights, travel and tourism law, culture and heritage, IP, communications technology law, competition law, China and World Trade.

He decided to leave the academic world behind to concentrate on artistic and spiritual development. He has exhibited paintings in a number of countries and has continued his writing in both fiction and non-fiction.

Made in United States
Troutdale, OR
05/16/2024

19926513R00108